PENGUIN AFRICAN LIBRARY
Edited by Ronald Segal

The Struggle for Mozambique

EDUARDO MONDLANE

Eduardo Mondlane was born in the Gaza district of Southern Mozambique in 1920. The first of his family to receive formal education, he went to a mission primary school but, as an African, entry to secondary school was barred to him. However he taught himself English and obtained a scholarship to a high school in the Northern Transvaal from where he went on to study social science at Witwatersrand University. Because of his political activities as an organizer of a Mozambican students' association he was deported back to Mozambique and then arrested and questioned by the police. He was eventually sent to continue his studies at Lisbon University but on an American scholarship. The police continued to harass him, however, and study became impossible. He managed to transfer his scholarship to the U.S.A. where he finished his B.A. in 1953 and went on to take M.A. and Ph.D. degrees in sociology at Northwestern University, Illinois. Research at Harvard followed and then a job in the United Nations Department of Trusteeship as a research officer. During these years he continued to study the political problems of his own country and in 1961 he revisited Mozambique to find that nothing had changed. He then left the U.N. and made open contact with existing political movements in exile. Convinced that unity was essential from the beginning, he was among those who helped bring the various embryo parties together and in 1962, in newly independent Tanganyika, a joint Congress was held. The Mozambique Liberation Front (FRELIMO) was formed and Dr Mondlane was elected President. Two years later the armed struggle was launched and since then areas of Northern Mozambique have been freed from Portuguese control. He made frequent visits to the liberated areas and in 1968, at the party's second Congress held in Northern Mozambique, he was re-elected President. Eduardo Mondlane was assassinated in Dar es Salaam on 3 February 1969. He left a wife and three children.

EDUARDO MONDLANE

The Struggle for Mozambique

Penguin Books

BALTIMORE · MARYLAND

Penguin Books Ltd, Harmondsworth,
Middlesex, England
Penguin Books Inc., 7110 Ambassador Road,
Baltimore, Maryland 21207, U.S.A
Penguin Books Australia Ltd, Ringwood,
Victoria, Australia

First published by Penguin Books 1969
Copyright © Eduardo Mondlane, 1969

Made and printed in Great Britain by
Cox & Wyman Ltd,
London, Reading and Fakenham
Set in Monotype Plantin

To the people of Mozambique

Contents

Plates

The photographs for these were taken by and are the copyright of *Basil Davidson* and *Anders Johansson* and are reproduced with their permission.

1 Dr Eduardo Mondlane, President of FRELIMO, at the Congress in Mozambique, July 1968.

2 Eduardo Mondlane at the opening of the FRELIMO Congress in the woodlands of northern Mozambique.

3 At the Congress. Left to right: Alfredo Aywasera, senior commissar of FRELIMO units in Tete Province; Samora Machel, FRELIMO commander of army; Francisco Manganja, military commander in Tete Province; Francisco Chisano, leading member of the FRELIMO executive committee.

4 The Women's delegation at the Congress.

5 Two guerrilla officers examining captured Portuguese weapons of West German and Belgian makes.

6 FRELIMO soldiers at a guerrilla camp in Cabo Delgado.

7 Guerrillas on the move.

8 Eduardo Mondlane with Uria Simango, Vice-President of FRELIMO, at the Congress.

Maps
1 Mozambique.
2 Tete Province.

Acknowledgement

Many people have contributed ideas, encouragement and work that have made this book possible; among them I'm grateful to Margaret Dickinson and Sérgio Vieira for gathering and arranging much of the research material.

of the day when the struggle was to start. We had sixteen weapons: six sub machine-guns, six rifles and four automatic pistols. We selected a group of twelve comrades, and left behind us some weapons for the defence of the base. On the morning of the twenty-fifth we arrived at the township of Chai. We went without our shoes for fear that we should be discovered because of our boots and followed. The township has a secretariat, the house of the *chefe do posto*, the house of the manager of Sagal (a cotton company), shops, a hospital, a prison and the houses of the policemen and of the white police.

We camped near the Lake of Chai. I told one of our comrades who was in uniform to put on civilian clothes and go out to reconnoitre the township. I put a bandage on his foot so that he could feign injury. He went out to the medical station in the post, stayed there some time and then went up to the secretariat. He got into conversation with an African who unknowingly revealed where the troops slept: the white soldiers slept behind the house of the *chefe do posto*; the officials slept in his house; the African soldiers slept in the secretariat. This Mozambican also told our comrade where the sentries were posted (on the veranda of the secretariat and the house of the *chefe do posto*). The guerrilla stayed a little longer, went round the house of the *chefe do posto* and the prison, then went back to the secretariat. He saw three lorries leaving, and learnt that they were going out on a hunting expedition. They went out hunting every day. After this every night one lorry would go on patrol. Our comrade came back with this information. I made a plan of attack. One machine-gun would neutralize the African troops in the secretariat. I decided to concentrate the attack against the house where the *chefe do posto* and the officials were. I gave each comrade his position for the attack. They were to stay camouflaged under the mango trees. At 16 hours we came out into the open; at 18 hours we were at the post, in our positions. The Portuguese were beginning to light the lamps in the houses. At 19 hours we advanced until we reached the house of the *chefe do posto*.

While we were advancing, the lorries that had been out on the hunt returned and came between us and the house. They unloaded the animals which had been killed. We watched their every movement. We were not seen. After they had unloaded, the soldiers got into the lorry and set off on the road to Macomia. The lorries disappeared – we decided they had gone on patrol. The guard came and stationed himself at the door of the house of the *chefe do posto*, seated on a chair. He was white. I approached the guard to attack him. My shot would be the signal to the other comrades to attack. The attack took place at 21 hours. When he heard the shots, the *chefe do posto* opened the door and came out – he was shot and killed. Apart from him, six other Portuguese were killed in the first attack. The explanation given by the Portuguese authorities was 'death by misadventure'. We withdrew. On the following day we were pursued by some troops – but by that time we were far away, and they failed to find us.

This small operation, reported here in the words of its commander, was one of the first battles in the war now being fought by the Mozambique Liberation Front against the Portuguese. It took place in the northern province, Cabo Delgado, in conjunction with other coordinated engagements, on 25 September 1964, to mark the beginning of the armed struggle. If events follow the course they have been taking in the four years since, that day may well go down as one of the most important dates not only in the history of Mozambique but in the history of the African continent.

Up to now relatively few people have seen and commented on the significance of Mozambique. The world press and even the African press rarely mention it. 'Portuguese' Africa has traditionally been an obscure part of the continent: the Portuguese did not welcome other foreigners, and even recently they have made it difficult for anyone to do serious research in the parts of Africa they control, whether in such subjects as social studies, economics and anthropology, or in the apparently neutral field of the natural sciences. The result is a dearth of information about these areas and especially about Mozambique, where the Portuguese themselves have done less work than in Angola.

A good illustration of the ignorance about Mozambique is this remark made in 1962, two years before the outbreak of war, by a man who had studied the Angolan situation in some detail:

'It can be argued that in some parts of Portuguese Africa, *particularly Mozambique*, Portuguese rule has maintained an atmosphere of peace and apparent contentment.'*

There are many people, reasonably well informed about the English and French speaking countries of Africa, who can scarcely place Mozambique on the map. If this is less common now than it was a few years back, it is mainly due to the white

---

*Andrew Marshall, *Angola: symposium*, Institute of Race Relations, 1962. (The italics are mine.)

settler rebellion in Rhodesia, which focused attention on the Port of Beira and located Mozambique as the country which lay between Rhodesia and the Indian Ocean. But even those who can now identify Mozambique exactly, as a long thin country stretched along the East Coast, between Tanzania and South Africa, rarely know much more about it, except perhaps that it is 'Portuguese'.

About this 'Portugueseness' there are innumerable misconceptions. The most common, largely the product of skilful public relations work by Portugal, concerns the 'non-racial' Portuguese. This illusion is dealt with at some length elsewhere in this book. Another is an exaggerated idea of the depth and antiquity of Portuguese influence in the area. It is true that Vasco da Gama, on his famous voyage, landed there in 1498, that subsequently sporadic visits were made by Portuguese ships, and some small isolated trading posts established. But the idea that these early traders found in East Africa a savage coastline and completely primitive people on which they could easily imprint their 'civilizing influence' is far from the truth. Arab traders had already visited and settled the coast for something like a thousand years, spreading Islam and some of their material culture among the people of the coast.

As for the interior, by the fifteenth century, highly organized and materially advanced Bantu states had grown up, states which were responsible for settlements like the great stone city of Zimbabwe. These people for centuries had relations with the Portuguese on their own terms, with Portuguese influence exercised through court intrigue and religious blackmail among their few converts rather than through any political or cultural strength in the area.

Perry Anderson in *Le Portugal et la fin de l'ultra-colonialisme** reports that in 1854 'Livingstone calculated that there were 830 whites in Luanda and only 100 in the rest of Angola. Thus, in the middle of the nineteenth century one can estimate that there were never more than 3,000 Portuguese nationals in the whole of Africa south of the Sahara.'

Even at the end of the nineteenth century the Portuguese had made very little impression on Mozambique. Oliveira Martins

* Paris 1963.

gives us this general description of the Portuguese possessions in 1890. 'To stand on guard – triggerless – on the walls of a ruinous bastion, alongside a customs house and a palace where bad and ill-paid officials vegetate, watching with folded arms the trade which foreigners carry on and we cannot; to wait every day the raids of the blacks, and to hear every hour the disdain and derision with which all African travellers speak of us – frankly it is not worth the trouble.'*

Before the 1961 explosion, Angola was also very much of an unknown quantity to people outside the Portuguese Empire. But the revolt and the subsequent reprisals became headline news for a time in the world press and raised Angola out of her obscurity. The war which started in 1964 in Mozambique has not had the same effect. For about a year the Portuguese were very successful in keeping a curtain of silence across what was happening. They allowed in very few reporters, and selected only those which they were sure would report their point of view. Then in 1965 they made a mistake. They allowed in Lord Kilbracken, and although at that time he clearly had little sympathy with FRELIMO, he did report truthfully what he saw. The result was a series of articles in the *Evening Standard* which described a state of full-scale guerrilla warfare. Since then most of the major European and American papers have at some time given it coverage, but these articles seem to have made little impression on public imagination. Now, four years later, most papers still refer to it as 'the forgotten war'.

Public interest in this field has lagged a long way behind commercial interest. Even in the 1930s, international business was beginning to wake up to the great economic potential in Angola and Mozambique. An English visitor, Patrick Balfour, remarked expressively, 'The Portuguese colonies are no longer altogether a joke.' For almost another thirty years, however, the Portuguese policy of restricting foreign investment prevented this interest from having much practical effect. By the end of the 1950s, the state of unrest in Angola was causing enough alarm in the government to bring about a general revaluation of policy. With the outbreak of hostilities in 1961 it became clear that, completely

* R. J. Hammond, *Portugal and Africa*, Oxford, 1967.

17

alone, Portugal might have difficulty in keeping her grip on Africa. An influx of foreign capital in her colonies would both relieve the financial burden and attract some political support from interested groups abroad. Thus, the old laws restricting foreign investment were abandoned in favour of an 'open door' policy, which produced a flow of foreign money. Now, with huge companies like Gulf, Firestone and Anglo-American rapidly extending their interests, the Portuguese colonies have become in the world of big finance something very far from 'a joke'.

The war in Mozambique, therefore, has been followed with considerable interest in business circles. At the end of 1967 the conservative French newspaper *Figaro* devoted two editorials to the question. Both drew attention to the position of Mozambique in relation to the economic resources of the rest of Southern Africa and to world trade routes. On 24 October 1967 General Bethouart wrote:

A century after the opening of the Suez Canal, the sea route to India and the Far East has returned to the Cape route. The event is important. It will not be temporary. Unable to take the new large tankers, Suez will also continue to be handicapped by the convulsions shaking the Arab world from Aden to the Yemen and to Cairo where the Russians are entrenched.

Faced with this situation the West must revise its policy towards South Africa and the Portuguese provinces which, through their great sea ports, control the outflow of the prodigious mineral, agricultural and industrial riches to be found in large quantities in that part of the continent.

David Rousset, on 8 November 1967, endorsed Bethouart's remarks about the new importance of the Cape route and elaborated on the effects:

One knew well enough that when South Africa exploded the world would shake, but no one thought of the event as near. On the other hand the war which was raging in the Portuguese colonies seemed to be without world-wide implications, Portugal being too small a piece on the chess board of the big industrial countries. ... The return to the Cape route gives a strategic value to the guerrilla in the Portuguese colonies. To see this one need only glance at a map.

Mozambique, Angola and Portuguese Guinea occupy key positions.

There the Portuguese are struggling with an enemy who is already strong, well led and integrated into an international machine. One can reasonably guess that as soon as the strategic value of these positions is clearly understood, they will get more attention and more effective aid. The Portuguese colonies are emerging from the position of metropolitan provinces. As a result the South African question is also posed in new terms. For the world balance has been modified.

The significance of Mozambique in the Rhodesia issue has been given remarkably little attention, although on 27 December 1967 the *Guardian* did point out:

The French have a much easier route into Rhodesia than trying the complicated business of routing oil through Beira. They just take it 400 miles down the coast to Lourenço Marques where nobody puts the least obstacle in their way.

It should have been self-evident from the geographical position of the two countries that the attitude of the Mozambique government must have an enormous impact on Rhodesia's ability to evade sanctions.

The questions raised by these articles must make it clear that, if the war in Mozambique remains forgotten by the general public, in certain circles it is being watched with acute interest. The interests brought into play by the war reach not only beyond Mozambique and Portugal but beyond Africa. It seems impossible that the war will remain 'forgotten' much longer. Already articles such as Bethouart's, speaking for the outside interested parties, are preparing the ground for intervention, predicting chaos and collapse of Western Christian civilization in the area, and hinting at the presence of the 'Bolsheviks' and the 'yellow hordes' behind it all. To prepare the moral climate, the 'role of Portuguese colonization' for the African is being eulogized; the story of the assimilation policy, paternalism and non-racialism, dressed up for display.

The purpose of this book is to show what Portuguese colonization has really meant for the African, to trace the true origins of the war, and to try to indicate what the struggle means to the participants and what is emerging from it in terms of new social structures which may help to mould the Africa of the future.

Introduction

Note: The account of the first combat given here comes from a semi-official report published in *Mozambique Revolution*, September 1967.

The personal histories quoted elsewhere come mainly from a series of interviews tape-recorded in one of our military camps by a member of FRELIMO early in 1968 and translated from the Portuguese. These FRELIMO interviews are indicated in the text by (F.I.). An exception is the life story of Alberto Joaquim Chipande, which was recorded in English by Basil Davidson at the Second Congress of FRELIMO, July 1968. This is indicated by (D.I.).

November 1968

Part One : Under Portugal

I Colonization — The Tradition

When the whites came to our country we had the land, and they had
the bible; now we have the bible and they have the land.
African saying

The Portuguese claim the right to control the parts of Africa
known as Angola, Mozambique, Guinea Bissau, the Cape Verde
Islands, São Tome and Príncipe islands. These African colonies
are practically all that is left of the empire which the Portuguese
established in the sixteenth, seventeenth, eighteenth and nineteenth centuries. Angola covers the largest area, but Mozambique
has the largest population (now probably about 8 million, although
official statistics give it as nearer 7 million).

Contacts between Portugal and parts of what is now known as
Mozambique began at the end of the fifteenth century, when
Vasco da Gama, the celebrated Portuguese navigator, reached
the island of Mozambique in early March 1498. Since the main
interest of the Portuguese kings who sponsored these trips was
in opening a safer route to India than the then dangerous Near
East land route, the Portuguese were satisfied for many years
with the provisioning stations they established along the East
African coast, and they left the rest of the interior untouched.
The Portuguese claim now that they have been in Mozambique
for over 450 years, implying that for all that time they have
controlled the country politically. If there is any truth in this
claim, it lies in the fact that soon after their first contact with the
people of the coastal region of East Africa, the Portuguese, envying
the wealth and power of the Arab rulers of the time, organized
whatever forces they could muster and fought their way into a
position of control. Taking advantage of the rivalries which
existed among the sherifs and sheiks of such city states as Pate,

Malindi, Kilwa, Zanzibar, Mozambique and Sofala, famous for their 'prosperity and elegance', they at last succeeded in monopolizing the then very rich trade in ivory, gold and precious stones.

In the city states, political development lagged behind material and cultural progress. According to Professor James Duffy: 'Political unity among these city states was a transitory burden. Each local prince defended his city's political and commercial independence, and at no time was there an East African nation, although the stronger towns at one time or another dominated their weaker neighbours.'*

Yet even though the Portuguese exploited this situation, they were never able to impose a lasting political control, except on a very thin coastal strip running from Cabo Delgado to the city state of Sofala. By 1700, a resurgence of Islamic influence in this part of Africa had been able effectively to eliminate Portuguese traders and soldiers, and to drive the Portuguese from scores of towns which they had held from time to time.

From the beginning of the eighteenth century, the Portuguese concentrated on winning control over the rich commerce of the area between Cabo Delgado and the Zambezi basin, in an attempt to capture the flow of gold from the then famous gold mines of Monomotapa, which they believed to be the proverbial 'King Solomon's mines'. In this instance, their activities affected an area which included what is today known as Zambia and Zimbabwe or Southern Rhodesia. The capital of Monomotapa's empire was located in Mashonaland and was part of the Makalanga confederacy of that time.

For 200 years, the Portuguese were thus able to derive a great deal of wealth from their control over the flow of commerce from the interior of the country to the coastal city states and abroad. During the seventeenth and eighteenth centuries, Portuguese authority was firmly established in the northern and central parts of Mozambique, so that it was possible to introduce Catholic missionaries, first Dominicans and then Jesuits, who introduced Christianity to East Africa. But whatever success this first missionary effort achieved, was almost completely destroyed in

* Duffy, *Portugal in Africa*, Penguin, 1962, p. 75.

the eighteenth century, by the corrupting effects of the alliance between the commercial, religious and political activities of Church and State.

This alliance between Church, State and commercial interests dates back to the very beginning of colonial expansion. In 1505, King Manuel gave an order to enslave the Muslim merchants of Sofala, 'because they are enemies of our Holy Catholic Faith and we have continual war with them'. The real reason for the expulsion, commercial competition, is openly admitted in a letter from Duarte de Lemos to the Crown, urging the killing or expulsion of 'respectable Moors' and exempting the Swahilis (although they were usually Muslim by religion), 'since they are like animals, and satisfied with gaining a handful of maize; nor can they harm us, and they can be used for any kind of work and treated like slaves'.* The split caused in the European Church by the Reformation was clearly a great blow to the Portuguese. Marcelo Caetano complains that 'the religious reformation also led to the dissolution of the Empire, since the countries which left the Roman communion failed to respect the pontifical bulls which, in exchange for missionary work, committed to Portugal the newly discovered lands and gave her exclusive sovereignty.'†

The Reformation may have diminished the usefulness of the Church as a political ally in international affairs, but at local level the Church remained a powerful force, and was rewarded for its work with grants of land which were exploited like any secular estate.

It was during the seventeenth and eighteenth centuries that the *prazo* system was introduced in Mozambique. *Prazeiros* were Portuguese white and Goan settlers and landowners who, not unlike European feudal lords, ruled those Africans who had the misfortune to fall under their authority and control. The lot of these Africans was worse than that of slaves. The *prazeiros* often controlled whole districts as personal properties, and recognized

---

*James Duffy, op. cit.
† Marcelo Caetano, *Colonizing Traditions, Principles and Methods of the Portuguese*, Lisbon, 1961.

no law but their own, only occasionally paying their vassalage to the King of Portugal. Jesuit and Dominican missionaries of the time also came to own vast tracts of land, administering them like any *prazeiro*, collecting head taxes and, when slavery became more profitable, dealing in slaves. It was out of the *prazo* system that the great land companies, such as the Niassa and Manica e Sofala, developed. The peculiarly Portuguese concessionary company system, which typifies the major economic enterprises of Portuguese colonialism, probably derived its refinements from the *prazo* system of this period.

Corruption in the *prazo* system was so rampant that, by the third decade of the nineteenth century, even the Portuguese government felt compelled to outlaw it. Its disregard for persons and property was notorious, and the slaving manor lords drove an excessive number of Africans away from the area altogether.

Most of such activities in East Africa took place primarily along the thin coastal strip, involving mostly communication with the Arabs and the Swahilis, and only very superficial contacts with the bulk of the Bantu-speaking people of present-day East Africa and Mozambique.

It is from the proverbial scramble for Africa, which began in the second half of the nineteenth century, that we must date the start of the Portuguese conquest of what is now Mozambique.

After the partition of Africa at the Berlin Conference of 1884–5, Portugal was impelled to capture and control what had been assigned to her. And in order to accomplish this, the Portuguese used every technique known in the history of colonial conquest. Where it was possible, she used infiltration by Portuguese traders, who disguised themselves as simple businessmen interested in the exchange of goods between equals; but subsequently, having thoroughly spied and mapped out a whole region, they sent in their military forces to wipe out any resistance from local rulers. At times the Portuguese used white settlers, who pretended that they needed land to farm, but who, after having been accommodated by the native traditional rulers, claimed possession of the communal lands and began enslaving their African hosts. Sometimes even Portuguese missionaries were used as 'pacifiers' of the natives, with the Christian faith offered as a lullaby, while the Portuguese military forces occupied the land and controlled the people.

Where the traditional political authority was strong, and the military machinery adequate in offering serious resistance to European conquest, the Portuguese were more tactful, using techniques of initial contact which were more gentle. They were prepared to begin their contacts with strong African states by establishing diplomatic relations, sending Portuguese 'ambassadors' to the courts of the most important traditional rulers. Then, after having sufficiently explored the internal strengths and weaknesses of the government, they proceeded to attack, using the traditional excuses of 'provocation' or 'protection of white settlers or missionaries'.

The war against Gaza, the last of the Mozambican traditional empires, was justified in this way. Beginning in 1895, it finished three years later with the death in battle of General Magigwane and the capture and deportation of the Emperor Gungunhana to Portugal, where he died several years later.

At the beginning of the twentieth century, the Portuguese began to set up their system of administration, although it was not until the early 1920s that armed resistance from the African population was finally crushed in all areas of the territory.

The men who were in charge of this campaign of pacification set the pattern for future colonial policy, establishing in the wake of conquest a system of administration which has changed little. During the previous century, theoretical colonial policy had fluctuated with political vicissitudes in Lisbon, but within the colonies, since Portuguese control was peripheral, these fluctuations meant very little. A liberal like Sà da Bandeira could legislate against slavery and outline more humanitarian principles; but he did not have, and could not create, the machinery to enforce his policies. It was only in the 1890s and 1900s that the Portuguese government had the power in Africa to develop a colonial policy which had some applicability.

António Enes was the most influential of those who supervised the pacification. Royal Commissioner of Mozambique in 1894–5, he was surrounded by a group of military men, many of whom followed him into the administration. Among these were

27

Mousinho de Albuquerque, who was fêted as a colonial hero in Lisbon for his campaign against Gungunhana, and who succeeded Enes as Royal Commissioner and wrote a work on the newly controlled colony, *Moçambique*, 1899; and Eduardo Ferreira da Costa, governor of Mozambique in 1896, Governor General of Angola in 1906, and author of *Estudos Sobre a Administração Civil das Provincias Ultramarinas*, which sets out the main principles of future colonial administration.

These men were all formed in a military mould, devoted Portuguese patriots with little time for the broader views of liberals. They were indignant at the humiliating way in which Portugal had been treated by the other colonizing powers. Enes' approach was straightforward and practical: the colonies were to be made useful, providing Portugal with profit and prestige. This meant that the conquest had to be completed, an administrative system established to secure the conquests, and then economic exploitation energetically pursued. The chief consideration was utility to Portugal; the concept of mission could be left to theorists and apologists. He was quite clear about the role of the Africans: like everybody else in the colony, they were to be turned to the purposes of Portugal. 'If we do not learn how to make the Negro work and cannot take advantage of his work, within a short while we will be obliged to abandon Africa to someone less sentimental and more utilitarian than we.'*

The keystone in the administrative structure was the Governor-General, who first wielded his power from the capital city of Mozambique in the north, and later from Lourenço Marques in the south. Under him were the various provincial governors; below these were the district *intendentes*, who supervised the administrators of circuits; these in turn had the duty to oversee the work of *chefes do posto*, each of whom directly controlled the daily lives of thousands of Africans in the country. To facilitate the work of the administrators and the *chefes do posto*, the Portuguese government re-established a limited traditional authority for several African chieftains. But in order to make certain that no one African ruler could ever acquire sufficient power to challenge the white man, the Portuguese government split the

* James Duffy, op. cit.

various chiefdoms into small territories, each with only a few thousand people. All African chiefs were made directly responsible to either the circuit administrator or to the *chefe do posto*. Even more important was the fact that the chief's power no longer derived from a concept of legitimacy within traditional society but was based on the conflicting concept of Portuguese legality. The chief was no longer the leader of his community but the representative within his community of a hierarchical colonial authority. The old political ties between the various African communities were severed, and their place taken by Portuguese power.

Having established complete political and administrative control, and having handed over to the Catholic Church the responsibility for spiritual 'pacification' of the people, the Portuguese government proceeded to distribute the natural resources of the country to the various economic interests which were vying to explore and exploit them. Such natural resources included agricultural land; the natural harbours of Beira, Lourenço Marques and Nampula; the five largest rivers of East Africa, all of which have their estuaries in Mozambique; all kinds of hard wood, rubber plants, palm trees, wild animals for hides and skins, fisheries, and above all, a large labour force.

The Portuguese government leased out large tracts of land to foreign companies, which not only acquired rights over natural resources, but were also allowed to control directly the lives of all Africans living within these leased areas. Consequently, vast territories in the central and some northern regions of Mozambique soon enjoyed a juxtaposition of governments: the Portuguese colonial authority, as represented by its governors, administrators and *chefes do posto*; and the local companies, which had ample rights to force all able-bodied men, and sometimes women and children as well, to work in their plantations at nominal pay.

To begin with there were three large companies: the Moçambique, the Niassa, and the Zambézia. All had the blessing and encouragement of the Portuguese government, and the first two had a formal charter. Each was assigned an enormous section of the country within which to explore and exploit mineral and agricultural resources, and set up the necessary lines of communication. In the area assigned to it, each had a monopoly on commerce, mining, construction, postal services and the right to transfer land. It also had sole right to collect taxes: the foundation of its power over the local population and its means of collecting labour. Indeed, the capital of these companies, partly Portuguese but largely foreign, was extremely small in relation to the areas allotted, an indication that exploitation rather than development was the intent and that any provisions for building schools and hospitals, or otherwise promoting the welfare of the population were not taken very seriously, if proposed at all.

The Moçambique company was given 62,000 square miles in the district of Manica and Sofala; the Niassa company was given the vast area of land north of the Lúrio river; and the Zambézia company was given the rich area of Quelimane and Tete, though in this case without the administrative rights. In fact, this last company prospered most, while the other companies found the task of administration, although executed incompetently and largely turned to their own advantage, a burden in the long run. The companies did not yield the large profits anticipated, but they did set a pattern for the future; extensive use of the concession, and cooperation between companies and administration in pursuing the same ends – profit for the companies and submission of the local population.

At the same time a number of smaller companies – most of them wholly, or partly, foreign-owned – came in to build the ports, the railways and to prospect for minerals in the south. But although these activities transformed the face of the colony, the effects did not reach very far. Again the expected profits did not materialize, and big international capital lost interest. The extensive mineral resources of Mozambique had not yet been discovered, and nearby South Africa, with its supplies of gold and other metals, was a much more attractive proposition.

Land remained the main source of profit. At the time of the Portuguese expansion, nearly all the land in Mozambique belonged to the various African peoples living in the area, with the exception of regions, particularly in the Zambezi valley, where the land had been expropriated earlier by the *prazeiros*.

In the late 1890s the three big companies carried out further extensive expropriations, converting the land mainly into plantations and estate farms for growing cash crops like sugar, sisal and cotton. Settlement was a separate aspect of land alienation. Civil servants and officials were encouraged to stay in the province, and efforts were made to import colonists directly from Portugal. For these schemes land was again taken from its African owners. A land policy was initiated in 1901, when all land not privately owned was declared to be the property of the State. Since the various types of African land tenure did not count as private ownership, this meant that virtually all land owned and farmed by Africans came under government control.

In theory the government set aside large tracts for the exclusive use of Africans, supposedly to safeguard traditional ownership. In practice, however, this stipulation was waived where a company or individual wanted land. At the beginning of the twentieth century, the government was unable to attract many Portuguese settlers, and pressure came mainly from companies and plantation owners. At that time, therefore, only a small amount of land was in fact alienated to settlers; but the policy of settlement was established, so that later, when a demand arose, large amounts of land could be seized for this purpose.

During this early development of the colony, agriculture and the search for minerals yielded relatively small profits. But there was one resource that could be profitably exploited: labour. It was on labour that all the other enterprises were founded; the exploitation of labour was central to the whole development of the colony.

*In the pre-colonial period, the slave trade had been the most profitable form of commerce in Mozambique, and the *prazos* had been based on slave labour. Thus it is not surprising that the system of slavery set the pattern for early colonial development.

Although our main concern is with the use of slave labour within Mozambique, there are some aspects of the traffic in slaves which are important. The first is its relative recency. In Mozambique the trade both reached its height and came to an end later than in most parts of Africa. The distance from American markets accounts for the slow start, while the demands from the French sugar islands led to a boom in the mid nineteenth century. The second is the history of its abolition, which bears on developments inside the colony. The initial movements against the trade came not from the Portuguese government but from the British, who were at that time trying to extend their interests, and possibly their territory, into areas of Africa under Portuguese domination. The result was a tendency for the authorities in Mozambique not to take abolition very seriously and to ignore or collaborate with the efforts of traders and settlers to continue the traffic in defiance of legislation by the distant metropolitan government. Moreover, legislative loopholes were left which allowed the same practices to persist under different names. In 1836, a decree was passed prohibiting the traffic in slaves; but the trade continued to flourish as before, with the only difference that the slaves might be referred to as 'free emigré labour' when necessary. In 1854 the status of *liberto*, or free man, was created, supposedly to provide the useful transitional stage between slave and free man; but in fact this only served to give official sanction to the practice of not calling a slave, a slave. For the *liberto* remained bound for a period of seven years and was subjected to a number of restrictions not dissimilar to those of slavery. And in 1866, for instance, the British commissioners from Cape Town reported that: 'At Ibo, Point Pangane, Matemo, Lumbo, Quissanga and Quirima, from 5,000 to 6,000 slaves were seen ready for embarkation . . . at the settlement at Pemba Bay the Cape Commission is informed that there is no traffic carried on except in slaves.'*

A similar situation arose when the government set about abolishing slavery on the estates within Mozambique. Attacks on the system followed soon after the first moves against the trade were made. A decree in 1869 made all slaves throughout the empire *libertos* but stated that they should be bound to their masters until 1878. In 1875 the status of *liberto* was abolished, but the ex-*liberto* was still obliged to contract his labour for two years. This half-hearted method of abolition tended to encourage

---

* R. J. Hammond, op. cit.

among the settlers the attitude that freed slaves could still be used as slaves. A clause allowing vagrant *libertos* to be forced into labour contracts also left a large loophole which was consistently exploited. In 1899, indeed, a decree was issued which gave official sanction to this smooth transition from slavery to forced labour. It stated that 'all natives of Portuguese overseas provinces are subject to the obligation, moral and legal, of attempting to obtain through work, the means that they lack to subsist and to better their social condition'. If the worker failed through his own efforts to do this, the government could intervene to force him under contract into either its own service or that of an individual employer. Naturally, with a ready source of cheap forced labour, there were few jobs available at a level of pay which could attract the African of his own free will, and since only Africans with unusually large and productive plots of land could claim exemption as farmers, the decree covered the vast majority of the adult population. Thus the African found himself dispossessed not only of his political power and his land, but also of the most rudimentary rights to control his own life. He could be treated virtually like a slave: forced to leave his home and family to work almost anywhere, for excessively long hours and for merely nominal pay.

If this pool of labour could be turned to good account in the plantations of Mozambique, it was found to be even more profitable if exported to the mines of the Transvaal. The need for labour was such that the mining companies were prepared to pay the colonial government a fee for each labourer sent. Various conventions were drawn up between the Union of South Africa and Mozambique, and in 1903 the Witwatersrand Native Labour Association was given full rights to recruit labour in Mozambique. While other enterprises had been largely disappointing, this export of labour at least brought in a steady profit, and it became firmly rooted in the colonial system as one of the mainstays of the economy.

Thus, in the years between 1890 and 1910, the main characteristics of Portuguese colonialism were established: a centralized net of authoritarian administration; the alliance with the Catholic Church; the use of companies, frequently foreign, to exploit

2 Social Structure – Myth and Fact

I believe that the great success in the relations of the Portuguese with the populations of other continents is the consequence of a *suigeneris* form of ethnocentricism. In fact, the Portuguese do not need to affirm themselves by denying . . . they affirm themselves through love. Here lies the secret of harmony prevailing in all the territories where Portugal settled.

Jorge Dias (a Portuguese ethnographer)

Our people have suffered a great deal. My parents, I myself, have been exploited. My uncle was murdered.

Teresinha Mblale (a Mozambican peasant [F.I.])

Most imperial régimes have tried to paint their activities in favourable moral terms for the consumption of public opinion. They attribute various virtues to their particular brand of colonialism, to differentiate it from the nefarious practices of their rivals. Portugal's special claim for her methods is the contention that they contain no element of racialism. To support this, statements and royal directives are quoted from as far back as the sixteenth and seventeenth centuries. For example, this royal order of 1763 declared: 'That it was my pleasure by means of an ordinance dated the 2nd April seventeen hundred and sixty one to revive the pious laws and praiseworthy customs which have been established in that State whereby all my vassals therein born, being baptized Christians and having no other legal impediment, should enjoy the same honours, pre-eminences, prerogatives and privileges that the nationals of this realm enjoy.'

Recently the greater interest taken in African affairs has led a number of Africanists, journalists and humanitarians to point out the falseness of this claim. Also, with the general acceptance afforded the principle of self-determination, Portugal has been subjected to considerable international criticism for her colonial policy. Her answer to this has been chiefly to reaffirm this image of the non-racial 'colour blind' Portuguese, in order to argue that as equal citizens of a greater Portugal the inhabitants of her colonies have no need for independence. A few years ago Dr António de Oliveira Salazar, then Prime Minister of Portugal stated: 'These contacts (in overseas territories) have never involved the slightest idea of superiority or racial discrimination. . . . I think I can say that the distinguishing feature of Portuguese Africa – notwithstanding the concerted efforts made in many quarters to attack it by word as well as action – is the primacy we have always attached and will continue to attach to the enhancement of the value and dignity of man without distinction of colour or creed, in the light of the civilization we carried to the populations who were in every way distant from ourselves.'

Gilberto Freyre, the well known Brazilian historian, has developed an elaborate theory of Luso-tropicalism to account for this 'distinguishing feature'. According to him, the people of Lusitanian (Portuguese) background were specially equipped by their Roman Catholic tradition, and by their long contact with people of various cultures and races, to cope peaceably with people of various ethnic and religious backgrounds. They were, so to say, pre-ordained to lead the world towards racial harmony and to build a far flung empire composed of peoples of various colours, religions and linguistic groups. He has developed this into a mystical theory of the essential Portuguese character: 'Portuguese success in the tropics is largely due to the fact that . . . their expansion in the tropics has been less ethnocentric, less that of a people whose activities are centred in their race and their deliberately ethnic culture system – than Christocentric – that is, a people who consider themselves more Christian than European.'

Yet even on the level of theory, the Portuguese have by no means been so solid on this point as the official line implies. In the 1890s colonial administrators such as António Enes, Mouzinho de Albuquerque and Eduardo da Costa made little effort to hide the inegalitarian and racialist basis of their views on the colonial question. Enes openly admitted: 'It is true that the generous soul of Wilberforce has not transmigrated into my body, but I don't believe I have in me the blood of a slaver; I even feel an inner fondness for the Negro, this big child, instinctively bad like all children – may all mothers forgive me – though docile and sincere. I do not consider him something to be exterminated because of the necessity for the expansion of the white race, although *I may believe in natural inferiority*.'* He was also a staunch supporter of authoritarian rule and forced labour: 'The State, not only as a sovereign of semi-barbaric populations but also as a depository of social authority should have no scruples in *obliging* and if necessary *forcing* these rude Negroes in Africa, these ignorant Pariahs in Asia, these half-witted savages from Oceania, to work . . .'

Even the statements quoted by the Portuguese themselves as proof of their lack of racialism, when examined closely show signs of the attitudes openly expressed by Enes and his contemporaries. In the royal order previously quoted, the phrase 'being baptized Christian' is crucial; the question of equality could only arise at all in the case of 'natives' who had made every effort to adopt Portuguese habits. Everywhere references to Africans in the context of their own society are full of scorn or at least pity: 'the natural simplicity of the people of this continent'. The implication is always that the Portuguese are naturally superior to the people they have conquered, and that these can only claim any sort of equality by actually becoming 'Portuguese'. In the meanwhile the role of the conquerors is described as 'a just, humanitarian and civilizing tutelage'. This is the policy of 'assimilation', which lies at the base of the Portuguese claim to non-racialism. The theory is that every inhabitant of the Portuguese Empire has the opportunity to absorb Portuguese civilization, and that if he does this, he will then be accepted on equal terms with those born Portuguese, irrespective of colour or origin.

Whether practice bears any relation to theory can be seen by a study of actual conditions in Mozambique. Unfortunately, any account of current social relations in Mozambique is hampered

* My italics.

at the outset by the lack of any comprehensive field studies made by outside social scientists, for the Portuguese government has always blocked the attempts to carry out such on-the-spot investigations. This in itself indicates how aware the authorities must be that the facts do not conform to their favoured image. Despite this opposition, a number of determined British and American scholars have been able to climb across the wall built by the Portuguese government and somehow gather enough information to supplement personal observations and experiences. For much of the background data, however, and particularly for population figures, it is still necessary to rely on Portuguese sources. This is scarcely satisfactory: first, because the census methods are far from accurate; secondly, because in accordance with the non-racial image, the authorities are unwilling to give a breakdown of figures by ethnic and racial groups.

The official 1960–61 statistics give the total population of Mozambique as 6,592,994. According to the *Junta de Investigação do Ultramar*, in its monograph *Promoção Social em Moçambique* (Lisbon, 1964), this population is composed of 'three distinct socio-economic strata'.

(a) A minority population, quantitatively about 2·5 per cent of the total population – composed of European whites, Asians, Mulattos and a few Africans concentrated in the urban areas and in the agricultural and mineral developments. It is a Westernized minority, and almost all of them are urbanized. They are employed in modern activities (enterprises), the State deriving a greater proportion of its public revenue from it.

(b) A numerical minority – 3·5 per cent, composed of elements of various races but above all of Africans, with a tendency to concentrate in the peripheries of the most important population centres. The Africans of this type of population are of rural origin, having the tendency either to attract to themselves distant family relations, or to detribalize themselves, thus abandoning, at least partially, the cultural and social habits of their origin. They turn, in general into a salaried (proletariat).

(c) A large majority – 94 per cent – of the Africans (we might as well say almost all of them) composed of the peasants, who live basically under a regimen of subsistence economy, complemented by some wage-work of a migratory nature and by some cash-earning peasant farmers. These are the residents of tribal regions, governed in their legal relations by traditional law.

Some figures for 1950 give a further breakdown of the first group into the following sub-groups:

Whites	67,485
Orientals	1,956
Indians	15,188
Mulattos	29,507
Assimilados (African)	4,555

The whites are numerically the largest sub-group. They also have a special position in relation to the other sub-groups in that most of them belong directly to the ruling nation and class. On the other hand the African, whether he belongs to the second or the third group outlined above, belongs directly to the conquered and colonized nation. Thus, it is the relationship between these two peoples which must be considered the basic relationship in the study of social structure. As in any society there are three essential aspects to be considered: the legal/political, the economic and the social.

The position of the 'native'

As we have seen, the background to the political relationship between the Portuguese and the African is one of conquest. The Portuguese sought to control the African either by influence, or failing this, through military conquest which directly destroyed the African political structure. The comments of the Portuguese, João Baptista de Montaury, give a fair idea of the nature of this relationship near the end of the eighteenth century: 'In general the Kaffirs of Sena, who are either slaves of the settlers or else tributary vassals of the State, are docile and friendly to the Portuguese, whom they call Muzungos. They dislike anyone who is not Portuguese. . . . This dislike derives from a superstitious fear that the Portuguese have spread among them, telling them that all Mafutos (non-Portuguese white foreigners) eat the Negroes, and other absurd tales which they implicitly believe. . . .

It is to be hoped that this conviction will endure in the minds of the said Kaffirs, for in this way we will always be able to dominate them and to live undisturbed. They are most obedient and submissive to their masters and to all Muzungos in general.'

It was not until the end of the nineteenth century, when conquest was completed and a comprehensive colonial administration set up, that the full legal basis of the relationship began to emerge. The significant point about the government established at the end of the nineteenth century was the clear separation of two administrative codes, one for Africans and one for Europeans. European areas were administered after the metropolitan model by the *conselho*, or council, with the area of the conselho subdivided into *frequesias*, or parishes; African areas or *circumscripções* were administered by the *chefes do posto* and his *administradores*, and subdivided into *regedorias* or chiefdoms, in which a chief, usually deriving his power rather from appointment by the Portuguese than from the original tribal structure, simply carried out the instructions of the *administradores*.

The main legislative achievements of the early twentieth century were to define the legal basis for this distinction between two types of population. The Native Assistance code of 1921 defined the civilized African as one who could speak Portuguese, had divested himself of all tribal customs, and was regularly and gainfully employed. He was to be regarded as a full Portuguese citizen, while all Africans not answering to this description were to be ruled under the *administradores*. This was the basis for the *assimilado* system, whereby the African population was divided into *assimilados* (assimilated), a tiny minority who had supposedly adopted an essentially Portuguese way of life, and the *indígenas* (natives), who formed the vast majority of the African population. The New State of Salazar, in the thirties and forties, continued this policy, elaborating and clarifying previous legislation. A *regime do indigenato* was set up in all the African territories. The African population was divided into two distinct categories, *indígenas* (unassimilated Africans) and *não indígenas* (anyone enjoying full Portuguese citizenship, including assimilated Africans, although in practice these were often regarded as belonging to a third category). The *indígena* had no citizenship, had to carry an identity card (*caderneta indígena*), and was subject to all the regulations of the *regime do indigenata*, which imposed on him labour obligations, excluded him from certain areas of the towns after dark, and restricted him to a few places of entertainment, including cinemas showing specially censored films. The *não indígena* had, in theory, all the privileges which went with Portuguese citizenship.

After the Second World War, substantial changes took place in the world outside. International organizations became more influential, the concept of self-determination was gradually accepted by most of the colonial powers, and there was a general movement towards greater democracy in many parts of the world. Portugal remained untouched by these tendencies until the Indian claims to Goa drew attention to the condition of her colonial territories, and Portugal began to feel the need to defend her colonial stand. She started negotiating to join the UN; but in order to do this successfully, she had to make some move to modernize the structure of her colonies. Her first action, in 1951, was to transform the colonies overnight into 'overseas provinces', making them an integral part of Portugal and so hoping to avoid UN resolutions relating to non-self-governing territories. The unrest in Angola, which in 1961 exploded into armed uprising, was a further impetus to change and allowed a group of government 'liberals', led by Adriano Moreira, to gain influence within the cabinet. The result was a series of reforms which culminated in 1963 with the publication of a New Overseas Organic Law.

The question of citizenship was dealt with in 1961 when, on 6 September, the *Estatuto dos Indígenas* was abolished, and all native inhabitants of Mozambique, Angola and Guinea were made full Portuguese citizens. It has, however, been a characteristic of the Salazar régime that government on paper bears little resemblance to government in fact: this case was no exception. The reform was made meaningless by the issue of different types of identity card to those 'citizens' who had previously been *indígen* and those who were counted as citizens before 1961. The former *indígena* holds a *Cartão de identidade* on which 'province of Mozambique' is clearly written and which inside specifies place of birth and residence in terms of native administrative area; the former citizen holds a *Bilhete de identidade*, which makes no mention of province or place of residence and which is in every respect identical to that held by a citizen living in metropolitan Portugal. Thus, in practice it is easy for the authorities to distinguish between these two classes of 'citizen', and the details supplied on the *Cartão de identidade* help police apply the old laws restricting the activities and mobility of the *indígena*.

The new Overseas Organic Law again in theory increased representation in the overseas provinces: it allowed for an extension of the municipality system, whereby local officials are elected on a limited franchise by the inhabitants of the area; and also provided for participation in the elections to the Central Legislative Assembly in Lisbon. There is a clause, however, which prevents this from applying to the African population. Section II of Article XLV states: 'Transitorily in regions where the economic and social development deemed necessary has not been reached, municipalities may be replaced by administrative districts, formed by administrative posts, except where the creation of parishes proves possible.' In practice, this means that all areas inhabited by Africans are governed by Portuguese officials under the old authoritarian system, but that a parish can be formed for a group of whites living within a predominantly African region.

The figures relating to the 1964 election in Mozambique show a very strong racial bias. Out of a total population of 6,592,994, there were only 93,079 qualified voters. Since the total *assimilado* and non-African population was 163,149, it is clear that not even everyone in this group had the vote and that therefore virtually no 'indigenous' African was enfranchised. In some districts there was a very close correlation between 'non indigenous' population and franchise:

	Local population	'Non-indigenous'	Voters
Manica and Sofala	779,462	31,205	31,054
Cabo Delgado	546,648	3,894	3,890
Niassa	276,795	1,490	1,489

In no district was the figure for voters higher than the figure for 'non-indigenous' population, although in many cases it was considerably lower.

It should be added that even for the very few people whom it affects, the law does not really provide for much local autonomy. By Article VIII, the system and scope of overseas governments are to be dictated by the National Assembly. By Article IX, the Governor-General of each province is appointed by the central government. By Article X, the Overseas Minister in Lisbon may 'cancel or abolish ... the legislative decrees of the overseas provinces if he deems them illegal or contrary to national interest'; by Article XI, the Overseas Minister 'nominates, demotes, promotes, transfers, etc., all staff of the general service of the overseas provinces'. Perhaps most important of all, by Article LX, general economic policy, including questions of settlement, displacement and labour, is drawn up by the central government. Clearly, even if in the future a significant number of Africans were enfranchised, they would not gain any worthwhile political power.

Since the African remains in effect without citizenship and divested of all political power, it would be surprising if this were not reflected in the continuing inferiority of his economic situation. The unassimilated African is by law severely restricted in his economic activities: he may not engage in any commercial activity, and he does not have the educational opportunities to enter a profession. Thus, the only way he can gain a living is by agriculture or wage labour. And wages are based on strictly racial considerations, as the following recent figures reveal:

Agricultural wages:

Race	Annual wage in escudos
Whites	47,723·00
Coloured	23,269·10
Assimilated Africans	5,478·00
Unassimilated Africans	1,404·00

Under Portugal

Industrial wages:

Race	Qualification	Daily wage in escudos
Whites	none	100.00 minimum
Coloured	none	70.00 maximum
Africans	semi-skilled	30.00 maximum
Africans	unskilled	5.00 maximum

To give an indication of what this means in practical terms, here are two brief accounts by Mozambican Africans of their own experiences. The first relates to an African with some skill, the ability to drive a car, and thus describes the condition of a fortunate minority:

Natacha Deolinda (Manica and Sofala Province): My father drove a lorry transporting loads of flour, sugar, rice, etc., for a company. . . . He earned 300 escudos a month ($10.17 cents) working every day and often the night as well, while the white lorry drivers earned at least 3,000 escudos ($100.17 cents) for the same work. . . . Life was difficult in our household: we ate a bit of maize, a bit of flour, sometimes a little rice, but it was very hard to buy meat; a very small piece of meat would cost at least 15.00 escudos. (F.I.)

The second account is by an ordinary labourer and describes work on the tea growing estate of the Sociedade de Chá Oriental de Milange:

Joaquim Maquival (Zambézia Province): My father earned, and still earns 150 escudos a month ($5.30 cents) . . .
The Portuguese wage-earners earned well. At the end of a month they would buy a new car,* while we couldn't even buy tea, and at the end of a year we didn't have enough to buy a bicycle. (F.I.)

For most Africans the only alternative to heavy manual labour is domestic work, but wages are low, with conditions hard and often humiliating. Another Mozambican describes her experiences:

Teresinha Mblale (Cabo Delgado Province): I was never able to go to school as we didn't have the money. I had to work and went as a maid to the administrator's house. They paid me 50 escudos a month ($1,75 cents). I had to start early in the morning and work through

---

* That is, would make the first hire purchase payment. This is quite possible: unskilled Portuguese earn more in the colonies, than in Portugal, and many do own cars.

44

till sunset, often into the night as well. I didn't get meals there. My bosses hit me and insulted me. If I broke a glass, they hit me and shouted at me, and at the end of the month I would not get paid. (F.I.)

The law itself sanctions this state of acute inequality. Such was implicit in the early legislation which allowed for a smooth transition from slavery to forced labour, but it was not until after the establishment of the fascist state in Portugal that the system was rationalized. On 6 September 1928, the 'Native Labour Code' was published in the form of a decree and was incorporated into the Colonial Act of 1930. Philippe Comte commented in 1964: 'The principle of discrimination was written into the name even of the 1928 law: there were two sets of labour regulations, one for natives, one for others, and the former imposed extremely hard conditions on the worker.' (*Revue Juridique et Politique: Indépendence et Coopération nos. 2–4 April/1 June 1964*.) Article 3 of the Code supposedly forbade the practice of forced labour, but added – 'without hindering the natives from accomplishing the moral duty of assuring themselves by work, of the means of subsistence, and in this way serving the general interests of humanity'. In effect, by its other articles the law makes full provision for a system of forced labour: Article 294 authorizes forced labour in exceptional cases, for urgent projects; Article 296 permits it in cases of urgency, or 'for any other reason', a phrase which takes all meaning out of the word exceptional in Article 294; Article 299 permits the use of force in recruiting labour.

The principle of forced labour is contained even in the Portuguese constitution, which states in Article 146, still in force today, that: 'The State cannot force natives to work except on public works in the general interest . . . to fulfil sentences of a penal character and to fulfil fiscal obligations.'

The 1928 Code itself, however, was abolished in the course of the reforms precipitated by post-war international pressure and the Angolan insurrection. As part of her efforts to escape from international isolation, Portugal signed the International Labour Convention and the Abolition of Forced Labour Convention in 1959. From then on, her own labour regulations had to conform with the requirements of these conventions; in 1960 some of the clauses giving administrators wide punitive powers were repealed, and minimum wages were raised. Also in 1961, the legal basis for compulsory cropping was removed. Since then, on paper, there has been no forced labour in Mozambique. But we have already seen how, during the whole history of labour conditions, there has been a long tradition of paper reforms which have made no difference to actual practice. In the northern areas of Mozambique, compulsory labour of all types was practised widely up to 1964, when the war effectively put a stop to it by forcing the Portuguese to withdraw.

In 1961 a commission of the ILO went to investigate allegations of forced labour in the Portuguese colonies and reported that it was unable to find adequate evidence of a direct breach by the government of the 1959 Abolition of Forced Labour Convention. Some of its findings, however, appear to contradict this conclusion: in Mozambique the commission interviewed only one group of road workers, and these stated that they had been ordered to work against their will by their *chefe do posto* (ILO Official Bulletin, Vol. XLV, no. 2, para. 389); on the docks at Beira one of the men interviewed had been sent against his will (ibid., para. 387); at the Sena Sugar estates, one group of workers interviewed 'stated that they were not happy there and it seemed . . . that they had been ordered to come by the native or administrative authorities' (ibid., para. 497). On the question of financial pressure, the Head of the Native Affairs Department himself stated that 'natives were required to pay their taxes, and if they were not rich the only way of obtaining the necessary amount would be by working . . . if the tax had not been paid, the person concerned was sentenced to corrective labour to work off the amount due' (ibid., para. 451). This evidence was found in spite of the fact that the commission spent only six days in Mozambique and only visited the more prosperous areas around Lourenço Marques, Beira and Quelimane. Furthermore, although the commission did on some occasions interview workers without any official being present, fear of the PIDE (the Portuguese political police) would still have had an unseen influence on all discussions.

In 1962 a new labour code was published, called the 'Rural Labour Code for the African provinces and Timor' (Decree Law 44,310, 27 April 1962). The principle of discrimination is no longer stated in the title, but in fact the law has application to the same people referred to in the old law as 'natives'. 'Rural' in the code stands for 'unqualified' – agricultural labourers, miners, factory workers, domestic servants, 'all labour whose services consist of the simple activities of the labour force'. In this way discrimination is retained in practice although eliminated in appearance. The same is true of forced labour. Article 3 of the Code, following tradition, abolishes forced labour yet again and states that penal sanctions can no longer be used to enforce contracts or the payment of the head-tax. This is meaningless in practice, however, since civil sanctions, the payment of compensation, remain, and the failure to comply with these can be punished as contempt of court with a prison sentence. A decree law of 29 December 1954 states that 'prison sentences served on natives can be replaced by sentences of hard labour on public works'. Thus forced labour can continue without breaking the letter of the new law.

It is clear from the whole body of recent legislation that the African in Mozambique is in economic and political subjection to the white man. Even the law provides for inequality, while actual practice goes far beyond this, to keep the African firmly in the role of a second class being whose whole function is to serve the Portuguese minority. It is only to be expected that social relations should reflect this. The recent expansion of the white population has made the existence of separate racial communities increasingly obvious. Since the thirties, Portugal has been very successful in her efforts to encourage immigration to the African territories, and between 1932 and 1960 the white population of Mozambique increased from 18,000 to 85,000. The result of this has been the development of a clear white group, separate from and superior to the rest of the population: the central areas of towns are white – the African population lives in slums around the edges – there are white cinemas, white restaurants, hospitals have separate wards for white people, and in Beira even the buses are segregated.

Assimilation

To counter charges of racialism the Portuguese regularly cite the position of the *assimilado*. Professor Caetano in his eulogy on Portuguese colonial methods writes: 'Although respecting the *modus vivendi* of the natives, the Portuguese have always endeavoured to impart their faith, their culture and their civilization to them, thus calling them in to the Lusitanian community.'* Assimilation is the official recognition of a man's entry to the 'Lusitanian community': afterwards he can legally use all white facilities and supposedly has the same educational and progressional opportunities. In order to gain this new status, a person must fulfil the following conditions:

1. He must read, write and speak Portuguese fluently.
2. He must have sufficient means to support his family.
3. He must be of good conduct.
4. He must have the necessary education and individual and social habits to make it possible to apply the public and private law of Portugal to him.
5. He must make a request to the administrative authority of the area, who will pass it on to the governor of the district for approval.

Already a certain racial bias appears, for to fulfil these qualifications a man must be considerably more 'civilized' than much of the white population who have citizenship automatically: 40 per cent of Portugal's population is illiterate, and many have insufficient means to support themselves. As one might expect this racial bias does not, in fact, vanish the moment an African gains official *assimilado* status. Salazar himself has said: 'It takes a century to make a citizen.' This attitude is reflected in the situation of an *assimilado* who, although he escapes some of the legal disabilities of the *indígena*, does not find himself in a position of equality with his white fellow citizens. First of all, his economic position is markedly inferior. The table of wage rates given earlier showed that there is a very considerable differential in salaries for whites and for assimilated blacks. This is aggravated by the prac-

* Caetano, op. cit.

tice, common enough in countries with an unofficial or semi-official colour bar, of grading Africans into inferior jobs and giving whites preference irrespective of qualifications. Even if an African does the same work as a white, his job will often be given a different title so that the income differential can be preserved. Here is one example of how this works:

Raul Casal Ribeiro (Tete province): I also worked in the mine store doing the accounts, where I earned 300 escudos ($10,17 cents). When a Portuguese came to do the accounts, he earned nearly 4,000 escudos ($142) and did less work than I had done. I was alone while he had an assistant, but he still earned thirteen times as much as I did. In fact, it was his African assistant who did all the work; he just signed it. The African got 300 escudos a month like me; the Portuguese got 4,000. (F.I.)

During his education, too, the *assimilado* finds himself at a disadvantage: he always has to do rather better than a Portuguese child. One girl, who was at technical secondary school in Lourenço Marques, commented: 'The Portuguese didn't treat the African and the Portuguese pupils in the same way. Sometimes the discrimination was quite clear. For instance, they always gave the Mozambicans lower marks.' (F.I.)

When I visited Mozambique in 1961, the principal of the Salazar High School himself admitted that staff did tend to mark down African pupils.

One fact making complete nonsense of the suggestion that *assimilados* can reach a position of real equality with whites is that in order to enjoy any of his privileges, an *assimilado* must always carry his identity card with him. A white will not be questioned; he holds his privileged position by virtue of his appearance.

If an *assimilado* is out after curfew, he will regularly be questioned by the police; if he cannot produce his card, he will be arrested. Many privileges cannot be asserted even with the identity card: an assimilated African is not, for instance, admitted to a white cinema; he may often not use white toilets – an African Roman Catholic Priest recently cited a case where he saw an assimilated school teacher actually beaten by a white station master because he had used the European toilet on the station.

Even the concept of 'assimilation' is not as non-racial and

liberal as its apologists suggest. It involves no acceptance of the African as an African. In return for the doubtful privileges already described, according to the law he must live in an entirely European style; he must never use his own language, and he must not visit unassimilated relatives in their own homes. One of the absurd contradictions of the system is that while not receiving the same treatment as a white, he is expected to identify completely with whites. One *assimilado* relates: 'By the end of secondary school, I was almost the only African left in class. I used to get lower marks than the Portuguese boys for the same work. My white companions could not see anything wrong in this. At the same time they used to talk in front of me about "those ignorant blacks", referring to unassimilated Africans, and they could not see how this could be hurtful to me as an *assimilado*.' The most that the *assimilado* system even sets out to do is to create a few 'honorary whites', and this certainly does not constitute non-racialism; visiting Malawian and Japanese diplomats have been given such a status in South Africa.

Apart from the other failings of the system, its final condemnation is to be found in the very few Africans it has affected: out of a population of over 6 million in 1950, there were no more than 4,555 *assimilados*. A system which touches only such a minute minority, must be considered virtually irrelevant.

Miscegenation

The other main prop to the myth of Portuguese non-racialism is intermarriage. The Portuguese claim that at times it has even been encouraged as official policy. In 1910, Vaz de Sampaio e Melo wrote: 'Miscegenation is the most powerful force of colonial nationalism. Given equality to the European under the law and admitted to administrative, religious, political and military positions, the mulatto comes to adopt exclusively the customs and language of the conquering nation, and they constitute the most profitable and appropriate instrument for the spread of those ethnic characteristics in the native society.' The result of this policy is a mulatto minority, after the Europeans the largest of the minority groups, and an important element in the super-structure of *não indígena* society, although its importance is qualitative rather than quantitative. The Portuguese tend to exaggerate the size of this community. In fact, in Mozambique, mulattos constitute only 0·5 per cent of the population, whereas in South Africa 8·5 per cent of the population is made up of the Coloured.

The existence of a mulatto community was a feature of Port-uguese territory from the early days of Portuguese settlement, when conditions were such that very few Portuguese women could be induced to accompany the adventurers, who filled this gap by taking African women as companions. At this time, certainly, the system did not involve much racial equality: the women were virtually never made legal wives, and were, according to contemporary accounts, treated as servants or slaves. The offspring did quite often inherit their fathers' wealth and position, but this was more a result of the assimilation of the Portuguese to the African than the reverse. The eighteenth century estate owners of the Zambézia resembled degenerate African chieftains more than Portuguese lords.

The present-day mulatto community, however, is mostly urbanized and educated under the Portuguese system. Legally they possess Portuguese citizenship, and in respect of education and jobs they enjoy a far greater degree of actual equality than the *assimilado* does. Superficially they appear well integrated into Portuguese society, but the superficiality of this picture is shown most clearly by the position of a first generation mulatto, the child of one Portuguese parent and one African parent. Even today it is miscegenation not intermarriage which is accepted. In Angola in 1958 there were only twenty-five mixed marriages of any sort. These broke down as follows:

White and black   1
Mulatto and black   4
Mulatto and white   20

In almost all cases it is the father who is Portuguese; relations between a Portuguese woman and an African male are not viewed with such tolerance. The African woman would not be his legal wife, but at best a mistress who is also a servant – taken for convenience when the man either cannot afford a Portuguese wife or has not had the opportunity to look for one – or at worst a prostitute or the victim of rape. In the former situation, the child has to reconcile two completely divergent upbringings: when very young, he lives mostly with his mother, often in the servants' quarters, and is brought up to some extent as an African child, while when he is older, his father will send him to a Portuguese school, take him into the Portuguese household, and expect him in every way to behave like a Portuguese child. Often, he spends the first part of his life reconciling these factors and then has to suffer a great change in his position because his father takes a Portuguese wife. When this happens, the child may either be disowned, thrown back completely on his mother, or kept in the family in a distinctly inferior position to the children of the Portuguese marriage, receiving only secondary consideration in all matters of his welfare and upbringing. If his father is a priest, as often happens, the child will at least be spared this later rejection; but then, from the beginning, separation between his father's and mother's households will be even more complete. It is not surprising that mulattos often find themselves resenting the Portuguese and yet being unable to identify with the African part of their culture. Brought up to consider their mother an inferior, they often do not even speak her language.

The resentment felt by mulattos against the Portuguese is not only based on the circumstances of their childhood. Portuguese policy towards the mulatto has a distinct element of racialism which is tied to the idea that miscegenation is a means of cementing Portuguese domination over the indigenous culture. It is part of this policy that while mulattos should be treated as Portuguese in many respects, this should not include opening to them all the same opportunities: the highest offices, the top appointments should remain in Portuguese hands. The Portuguese anthropologist Mendes Correia gives a clear exposition of this: 'As human beings, tied to our race by the sacred bonds of origin, the mulattos have a right to our sympathy and help. But the reasons which we have propounded do not permit the political role of the *mestiços* to go beyond the limits of local life. However brilliant and effective may be their professional, economic, agricultural or industrial action, they, as naturalized foreigners, must never hold high posts in the general politics of the country, except perhaps in cases of proved and complete identification with us in temperament, in will, in feeling, in ideas, cases which are both exceptional and improbable.'

Thus both in his childhood and in his adult life, the mulatto has many experiences which are likely to prevent him from identifying himself completely with the Portuguese. It is chiefly the most educated mulattos, the intellectuals, who have been able to give expression to this: they were very much involved in the early anticolonialist political agitation and in the early manifestations of nationalism; and more recently, some mulattos have thrown themselves whole-heartedly into the present nationalist movement. Yet their very privileged position in relation to the African has hampered political activity, even political thought. They may have wanted to voice the protest of the mass of the population but have been far removed from it. For there is a division even deeper than that which usually separates a politically conscious intellectual from the proletariat he theorizes about; they often do not even have a common language. As a result they have tried very hard to return emotionally to their African origins, the African side of their culture. This can be seen in some common themes of the poetry of Craveirinha, Noémia de Sousa and the early work of Marcelino dos Santos: the black mother-figure representing their own African mother; Africa itself, the mother country; and a certain poetic fusion between the two ideas. Noémia de Sousa, for instance, writes, in a poem called 'Black Blood':

My Africa, strange and wild
My virgin raped
My mother!

How long have I walked
exiled from you, a stranger distant and self absorbed
In these city streets, pregnant with a foreign race?
Mother! Forgive me!

Mother! my mother Africa
of slave songs in the moonlight
I cannot CANNOT deny
the black, the savage blood
you gave me

For strongest of all in me
it floods my soul, my veins
through it
I live, I laugh, I endure
     MOTHER!

This attitude of mind expresses the present dilemma in which
the mulatto finds himself. On the one hand he is able to reach a
position of considerable eminence within the Portuguese framework; many of the best known Mozambican intellectuals are
mulattos, and the artistic life of the country, in particular, is
dominated by men such as José Craveirinha. On the other hand,
when they reach a certain level in their professions, they find the
door to further advancement shut in their faces, and if they protest
against this or start to take an active interest in the political affairs
of their country, they find themselves distrusted and subjected
to some form of repression. They early on began to think in terms
of nationalist revolt, but their distance from the ordinary African
population left them without the basis for converting these
ideas into realistic action.

Asians and Europeans

The remaining significant non-white minority is the Asian,
composed mostly of Indians together with a few Pakistanis.
The original Arab population of the coast to a large extent
integrated itself with the local Africans, and those who have
retained a distinctive character belong to a peripheral trading
group, in many ways similar to a part of the Indian community.
There is, indeed, an important division in the Indian community,
separating it into two groups with a different character and social
role. First there are the Indians or Pakistanis from the traditional
sub-continent. These are mostly Hindu or Muslim by religion,

usually run small-scale commercial ventures – bush trading stations in the country, small shops in the towns – and constitute a relatively closed community, which does not have close contacts with Africans, Europeans, or even the members of other Indian sects. In general, they are very similar to Asian groups elsewhere in East Africa and are equally peripheral to the political life of the country. The other group of Indians are the Goans. In the nine-teenth century, Portugal was unable to achieve much European settlement in Mozambique, but was very successful at persuading Goans to immigrate there. The tiny colony of Goa had been sub-jected to far more Portuguese influence than any African territory, and these immigrants were in many ways more Portuguese than Indian: they spoke Portuguese and in some cases had even adopted it as the language of the home; they were predominantly Roman Catholic. They were accordingly considered 'useful civilizing agents' by the Portuguese, and many of them were recruited for the civil service. Now there are still a large number of Goans in the administration, while there are also many in the various professions, particularly medicine and law. In theory, as in the case of the mulattos, all Asians carrying Portuguese passports have the same rights and opportunities as European Portuguese citizens; but in practice there are similar limitations to the 'equality'. On the whole, though, less friction results, partly because the family situation of the Goan is usually more settled, partly because assimilation was very much more effective in Goa than in Africa, and partly because the power of the Catholic Church in the Goan community is enormous. This means that those who have reacted against the Portuguese, and there are a number of Goan intellectuals who have given vigorous support to nationalist movements, more often than not find themselves opposed not only to the Portuguese but to their own community and even their own families.

The white minority itself is composed, on the one hand, of officials, administrators and military personnel sent out from Portugal for a time specifically to serve the government; on the other hand, of permanent settlers, mostly Portuguese in origin but with a sprinkling of Greeks, Italians, Afrikaners and other nationalities. It is government policy to encourage members of the first group, particularly the ordinary soldiers, to stay in the colony by offering them grants of land, and so some of these become settlers after their term of service is completed. The second group is rather different from comparable small white minorities elsewhere in Africa in that, although members of it monopolize nearly all the important jobs in business and the professions, a large part of it is engaged in fairly menial pursuits: there are white artisans, white small-scale farmers, even white labourers. The reason for this is to be found in the low level of education and the widespread poverty in Portugal itself. Many of the immigrants to the colonies were poor peasants in Portugal; 50 per cent of immigrants are illiterate, and an even higher proportion unskilled. In considering the character of Portuguese colonialism, Gilberto Freyre makes a virtue of this, claiming that because of their own poverty and rural background, Portuguese immigrants were able to mix easily with people of the colonies and did not have an innate sense of superiority.* This is not, however, substantiated by the experience of Africans in Mozambique. Portuguese settlers have often surpassed the government in their racialist approach. At Tete, in 1948, for example, when, for the first time the authorities allowed the children of non-whites to attend the local primary school, the white *colonatos* protested vigorously; and when their protest brought no result, they insisted that two rows of desks should be left empty to separate their own children from the non-white ones. Very recently in a *colonato* where the government had settled one or two Africans with whites, the whites harrassed the Africans and on at least one occasion beat up one of them, damaged his house and threatened his wife. These and the many similar events I have witnessed or heard of may be isolated incidents; but the grounds for friction are built into the system. Even if the new Portuguese arrivals are little or no better off than many Africans at first, wage differentials, preference in jobs and special government assistance in farming can hardly fail rapidly to change their situation and outlook. Even the poor illiterate peasant does a great deal better in Mozambique than he would in Portugal. Moreover, the very fact that many whites are uneducated and, on arrival, poor, brings them into **direct**

* Gilberto Freyre, *Portuguese Integration in the Tropics*, Lisbon, 1961.

competition with the African. For them, the African is a potential threat; for the African, there is no rational justification for the superior position of the white.

Since within the fascist system there is no democracy, even for citizens with full legal rights and the vote, there exists a certain friction between even the whites and the authorities. Because, however, it is the government which guarantees the white his privileged position, very few settlers have identified with the Africans in demanding independence. In some cases, as already indicated, the friction arises because the settlers want even stronger measures against the Africans, a greater degree of segregation. In others, they simply demand a greater degree of freedom for their own minority. At one time, there was in Mozambique a body of white liberal opposition to the establishment of the fascist state, just as there was in Portugal, but this has been virtually silenced now. There are a few, mostly intellectuals, whose anti-fascist convictions and opposition to Salazar are fundamental; who support the liberation movement; and of whom one or two have actually joined the resistance. In some areas of the fighting now, the government has found it necessary to punish ordinary white civilians for not showing enough active opposition to the guerrillas. Thus even the white minority is not a homogeneous body, identified in every way with the colonial government.

3 Education and Submission

Schools are necessary, yes; but schools where we teach the native the path of human dignity and the *grandeur of the nation which protects him*.*

Pastoral letter of Cardinal Cerejeira, Patriarch of Lisbon, 1960

It has been customary among Europeans and Americans to conceive of all human thought as deriving from the Western mind. Africa in particular was thought to have made no contribution to human development, was regarded as a closed and completely backward world only brought into the mainstream of development as a result of the European invasion. More recent scholarship, however, has shown this to be a product of the introversion and ethnocentricism of Western thought. Mr Leakey's work has pointed to Central and East Africa as the possible birth-place of human society in its earliest form.† In much more recent times, five or six thousand years ago, it was in the Nile valley that what we refer to as 'civilized' society first developed. While Europeans were still living in primitive tribal societies isolated in the Northern forest belt, North Africans were learning to control their environment, developing technology and science and forming a complex, settled society. They used mathematics to measure the land, to chart the movements of the stars and to design large elaborate buildings; they invented some of the earliest techniques of mining, iron smelting and casting; they took some of the first steps in the medical sciences. It was this society that absorbed the first primitive Moslem invaders and by a cultural fusion created the advanced Islamic culture of Africa, from which Europe gained many of the scientific ideas that made the Renaissance possible. Nor was it only areas of

* My italics.
† *Adam's Ancestors*, Methuen, 1934.

58

Islamic influence which could boast an advanced material culture. It is known now that some of the cities of West Africa and the Congo were built before the adoption of Islam. And if for the last five or six centuries Africa had ceased to be in the forefront of development, it was not even then a 'closed continent'. There is evidence of considerable trade and cultural exchange both between different areas of Africa and between Africa and such areas abroad as the Middle East and India.

While archaeologists and historians have shown the historical fallacy of the 'Dark Continent' thesis, sociologists have attacked other aspects of it. Europeans supposed that, because Africa was backward at the time they invaded it, Africans had no culture at all, no morality and no education. It is now realized that there were a number of cultures in Africa, some more complex than others but all embracing some kind of morality and all including some method of education through which children could absorb the culture and become well-adjusted members of the society into which they were born.

This is all sufficiently recognized now in most parts of Europe and America, and there is no need to argue the point any further here. But the recognition outside a narrow circle of experts is largely a product of the post-colonial period. To a colonial government the notion that the culture of the colonized either does not exist or is worthless is obviously convenient – too convenient to allow mere science to correct it.

Colonialists in general have despised and dismissed traditional African culture and education. They assailed it, instituting completely out of context a version of their own system of education, which would uproot the African from his past and force him to adapt to colonial society. It was necessary that the African himself should acquire contempt for his own background. In the Portuguese territories, education for the African had two aims: to form an element of the population which would act as an intermediary between the colonial state and the masses; and to inculcate an attitude of servility in the educated African. These aims are clearly expounded in a pastoral letter of 1960 by Cardinal Cerejeira:

59

We try to reach the native population both in breadth and depth to (teach them) reading, writing and arithmetic, not to make 'doctors' of them. . . . To educate and instruct them so as to make them prisoners of the soil and to protect them from the lure of the towns, the path which with devotion and courage the Catholic missionaries chose, the path of good sense and of political and social security for the province . . . schools are necessary, yes, but schools where we teach the native the path of human dignity and the grandeur of the nation which protects him.

At all levels, the schools for Africans are primarily agencies for the spread of the Portuguese language and culture. Broadly, the Portuguese ideal has been that carefully controlled education would in time create an African people speaking only Portuguese, embracing Christianity, and as intensely nationalist Portuguese as the metropolitan citizens themselves. If all the Africans in Angola, Mozambique and Guinea (Bissau) became Portuguese nationals, the Portuguese have dreamed, there would be no threat of African nationalism. But in 1950, only 30,089 Africans* in Angola and 4,554 in Mozambique had reached the legally recognized state of assimilation into Portuguese culture.

In implementing these policy objectives, the Portuguese government has decreed that only one language, Portuguese, is to be taught in schools under its jurisdiction in Africa. African languages are used chiefly as a means of facilitating the teaching of Portuguese, but even this is rare. Whatever the long-range prospects for this approach, the intermediate result has been the creation of a small class that looks down upon its own traditional languages and culture, but is not sufficiently educated to use Portuguese efficiently.

On the assumption that political unity is founded upon a moral unity, the Portuguese have attached great importance to religion in African education. The constitution of Portugal specifies a preference for Catholicism among religious faiths; 98 per cent of the people of metropolitan Portugal are Roman Catholic, and Portuguese law and practice in recent years have largely restored

* This figure includes families of Africans and mulattos (called *mixtos*).

the pre-republican unity between Church and State.* On the assumption that the establishment of a spiritual link between the motherland and its overseas territories is vital to the establishment of the desired political coherence, the Salazar régime has encouraged the diffusion of Catholicism in Africa and has turned over the elementary education of Africans to government-subsidized Roman Catholic mission schools.

School systems

There are two categories of school system in the Portuguese Territories: (1) the Roman Catholic mission schools, whose principal function is to educate Africans through the primary level: and (2) the more sophisticated government school system, catering for the whites, Asians and *assimilados*. The schools for Africans are organized as follows:

Ensino Rudimentar, (called *ensino de adaptação* after 1956, or *ensino Missionario*). According to law no. 238 of 15 May 1930 and to the Concordat of 1940, the aim of this 'rudimentary' education is to 'lead the *indigena* gradually from a life of savagery to a civilized life'. This programme is officially the responsibility of the Roman Catholic missions, although some Protestant missions are permitted to operate a few schools also. The school years are: *iniciação* (kindergarten), *primeira classe* (first grade), and *segunda classe* (second grade).

Ensino primário – This programme is for students who have passed the *ensino de adaptação*. It comprises *terceira classe* (third

---

* Portugal was officially secularized after the overthrow of the monarchy in 1910, but the separation of Church and State was never entirely effective. By 1919, subsidies had been restored to Catholic educational institutions. In 1926, when the present authoritarian régime took control after a decade of violence and instability, the special role of the Church in the civilizing of Africa was given legal status. By the Colonial Act of 1930, Catholic missions were accorded a privileged position among religious groups, on the grounds that Catholicism represents the national faith of Portugal and is therefore the logical 'instrument' of civilization and national influence. The Missionary Agreement of 1940, supplemented by the Missionary Statute of 1941, restored paid compensation for all property confiscated by earlier régimes and emphasized the national character of the Catholic missions. A 1941 decree prohibits the granting of subsidies to other than Portuguese Roman Catholic missions.

grade), *quarta classe* (fourth grade), and *admissão* (preparation for admission to the *liceu* programme).

The schools for Europeans, *assimilados* and others are organized along the following lines:

Ensino primário (primary education), a five-year programme (since 1952, when the fifth year was added) whose last year is prescribed for entrance to the high-school programme,

ensino liceal – including the *primeiro ciclo* (two years), the *segundo ciclo* (three years) and the *terceiro ciclo* (two years). The third cycle is designed for those preparing to enter a Portuguese university.

Prior to 1940, all school curricula for Africans were determined by the Department of Education and Instruction in the Territory; examinations were conducted by the State, and certificates were awarded solely by the Director of Education. Then, from 1940 to 1960, the Catholic Church officially took charge of preparing the curricula, and the examinations were conducted and certificates awarded on Church authority.

Preparation of the curricula is now in the hands of the Ministry of Education in Lisbon, in line with the 1950 reorganization of the African colonies into provinces of Portugal, and inspectors from the territorial office of the Director of Public Instruction pay periodic visits to the mission schools. It is clearly understood, however, that no government inspector may visit a Catholic school without the permission and cooperation of the proper religious authorities. For all practical purposes, the office of the Archbishop of Lourenço Marques is the centre of educational authority in Mozambique, as the office of the Archbishop of Luanda directs African schools in Angola and São Tomé. In all schools for Africans in Angola, Mozambique and Portuguese Guinea, the curricula are uniform except for a few local variations.

In practice, the three stages of education – rudimentary, primary and secondary – are organized to present a series of barriers to the African child seeking higher education.

The *ensino de adaptação* programme, the equivalent of kindergarten and the first two grades in most other African territories, is designed in theory to introduce African children to the Portuguese language and the beginnings of the three R's, so bringing him to the level of the Portuguese child starting primary school. In many country areas, however, the children of mulattos and Asians have been forced to go through the three years of rudimentary schooling although they were brought up speaking Portuguese and could have started primary school on the same level as Portuguese children; while in other areas, children of Asian or non-Portuguese European parentage, who have not been brought up speaking Portuguese, are allowed to start at a state primary school. Since the teaching is done in Portuguese from the first, many African children are unable to pass the *adaptação* examinations (normally given after three years of instruction) until they are twelve to fourteen years of age. Since the maximum age for entry to primary school is set at thirteen, a very large number of children accordingly find themselves debarred even from primary school.

The *ensino primário* programme – that is, the third and fourth years – covers materials similar to those used for Portuguese children at the same level. Content analysis of the textbooks used indicates that the focus is entirely on Portuguese culture; African history and geography are totally ignored. Emphasis is on the Portuguese language; the geography of Portuguese discoveries and conquests; Christian morals; handicrafts; and agriculture.

Beyond the fourth year, there is a class where students are theoretically prepared for either high school or industrial and technical schools. Very few mission schools actually have this fifth-year programme, however, so that the opportunity for an African child to gain the necessary qualification for entering secondary school is almost nil, unless he moves to the city and attends there a private school that can prepare him for the admission exams to the secondary programme. Another age barrier is encountered at this stage. The maximum age for entry to secondary school is fourteen, and it is rare that an African child has started his schooling early enough to have completed the three years of rudimentary school and the five years of primary school by the time he is fourteen.

Although over 98 per cent of the white Portuguese living in the African territories are Catholics, the government has retained control of the schools catering to the educational needs of whites,

Asians and *assimilados*. Children from these groups may attend either State-owned schools, or private schools, but curricula and examinations are, in both cases, supervised by the State. These State schools for Europeans are administratively directed by the Ministry of National Education in Lisbon. Within the Ministry education in Portuguese Africa and Asia is supervised by the Department of Overseas Education. There is a Division of Education for Mozambique, one for Angola, and one for Guinea and the islands, each headed by a territorial director. Each director is assisted by two inspectors, one for primary schools and the other for school health.

Education is compulsory for all European children who reside within three kilometres (about two miles) of a school and who are between seven and twelve years of age. Although the pre-scribed age of entry into primary school is seven, children may be admitted one year earlier. The curricula of the State schools are the same as that of all Portuguese schools at the same level in metropolitan Portugal, except for some minor adjustments to local geographic, climatic and social conditions.

A considerable number of European and Asian children, and a very few African ones, attend private schools supervised by the government. These schools – all Catholic in orientation, since Protestant schools are generally forbidden to receive Europeans – do not discriminate against Africans; but only a few Africans can afford to send their children there. The average tuition fee is roughly equivalent to $17,50 cents a month, and most of the African students are necessarily boarders, which raises the cost to a prohibitive level even for middle-class African parents.

Teacher training

The same dual standards that apply to the educational process in the Portuguese territories are carried over into the training of teachers for African and European schools. When the Catholic missions took over the education of the unassimilated Africans in the 1940s, the training of teachers for these African schools also became the function of the Church. The government Normal

School in Mozambique, which was closed down after the passage of the Missionary Act in 1940, reopened in 1945 as a Catholic rather than a government institution. Prior to that time, African teacher candidates needed only to complete the fourth grade to be eligible for admission to the training school, but now membership of the Catholic Church is also a prerequisite. Teacher candidates for the African rudimentary schools are drawn largely from unassimilated Africans.

In 1960, there were four of these teacher-training schools in Mozambique, operated by the Church and subsidized by the government; total enrolment was 341 male students, with some 65 graduates per year.

Staff for the government-operated primary and secondary schools catering to the 'civilized' population of Mozambique and other Portuguese colonies come from metropolitan Portugal. It is, however, possible for an individual who has completed the first cycle of high school to obtain a teacher's certificate qualifying him to teach in the lower grades in the private schools.

Results of the system

If the system is to be judged according to its professed aim of educating the African to Portuguese civilization, it must be admitted a failure. Very few Africans receive any schooling at all, with the result that in Mozambique between 95 and 98 per cent of the African population are illiterate. Most of the education they do receive is provided by Church bodies. In 1955 there were 2,041 rudimentary schools, with a total of 242,412 pupils. Of these schools 2,000 were run by Catholic missions, twenty-seven by Protestant ones, twelve by the government, and two were private schools. In 1959, there were 392,796 children receiving *ensino de adaptação*, but of these only 6,928 managed to start primary school.

Although nearly 98 per cent of the population of Mozambique is composed of black Africans, only a small proportion of children attending primary school are African, while the number of Africans in secondary school is almost negligible. In 1963 there were 311 primary schools catering for 25,742 pupils, but of those only one-fifth were African. In the same year there were only three State secondary schools which could award the school-leaving certificate. (There are three lower secondary schools.) These three State schools were educating 2,250 pupils, while the three main private secondary schools had 800 pupils. Of this total, only 6 per cent were black Africans. In 1960, at the largest academic secondary school in Mozambique (Liceu Salazar in Lourenço Marques), there were only thirty African students out of a total of more than 1,000. The Roman Catholic Church, which enjoys the responsibility for educating the native people, does not have a single secondary school for Africans. Some of the Protestant missions, which are still allowed limited facilities for working in Mozambique, subsidize and administer boarding houses for some of the very few African students who attend secondary schools in the capital city of Lourenço Marques. There are also a number of private secondary schools and a number of secondary technical schools, but with a very small number of African students attending them, due to the high fees required. One girl who did manage to get to a technical secondary school describes the conditions of her schooling:

Josina Muthemba (Gaza Province): My parents made a great many sacrifices to send me to school. I went to commercial school for five years. My parents had to save on food and clothes. At the primary school there were only about twenty of us Africans to about a hundred Portuguese. At the commercial school there were about fifty Africans to several hundred Portuguese. (F.I.)

Josina was in a very much more fortunate position than most Africans, as her father earned an exceptionally high salary for an African – 3,000 escudos ($142) – yet still her family could only just afford the fees. The State clearly did not encourage those who could not afford them: 'Out of the fifty Africans at the commercial school, not twenty had scholarships, while at least half the Portuguese had them, although their families were better off than ours.' (F.I.)

The government has also established university general studies at Lourenço Marques, but according to the information at hand, out of the 280 students enrolled in 1962, there were not yet a dozen African ones. There are a few Africans now attending university in Portugal itself, and a few taking some higher professional courses at technical schools in Portugal. But their number is insignificant in comparison to the hundreds of Mozambican white and Asian students in the same programmes. Every year, white Portuguese students cross the borders to South Africa and Rhodesia for their studies. This, of course, no Africans are allowed to do, even though some Africans manage to slip through and clandestinely register as local native students.*

Since 1963 there has been a considerable expansion in the number of schools. This is partly due to the settlement policy and an increase in the white population, but also to the war and an effort by the Portuguese government to win some African support. The *Boletim Geral do Ultramar* of 1967 gives the following figures for 1965–6:

	Schools	Teachers	Pupils
Primary	1,305	2,912	92,002
Academic secondary	46	530	9,028
Technical secondary	41	734	12,273

These include a large number of private and religious institutions not included in the 1963 figures, while the secondary school figures include also teachers' training, nursing courses, etc. The numbers being educated at State secondary schools have increased only moderately in the last four years. Unfortunately, there is no guide to the proportion of African students at the various levels; but reports by students recently escaped from Mozambique indicate that the proportions have been little affected by the expansion, except that considerably more Africans are now in technical institutes. For the ordinary African child in the country, the prospects of reaching even primary school are still very remote.

Apart from the sheer lack of schools and places, there are several

* That is how the author managed to get his secondary and part of his university education in South Africa. But when the Portuguese and South African governments found out, he was expelled from South Africa, and so from his university.

factors which prevent more African children from getting some schooling. There is the maximum age of entry already described. And there is money. Even the rudimentary schools charge fees, and although these may be less than $20 a year, this is a good deal more than a peasant or a plantation worker can afford, as he would probably earn after tax not more than $50 a year, and might earn less than $20. Even a man with a little skill, a driver or a clerk, earns not much more than $100 a year, after tax.

Higher up the academic scale, schools become progressively more expensive, while the incidental expenditure also increases. At the rudimentary stage, the parents may only have to buy the child some clothes; but later they will have to pay as well for various school materials, for transport and possibly for board. At the level of secondary schooling, transport and board pose considerable problems; most of the Africans live in the country while all the secondary schools are in towns – of the three upper secondary schools, two are in Lourenço Marques, one in Beira – and the schools make no provision for children from poor families who need to board cheaply. Finally, there is the quality of elementary education provided for Africans: as has already been pointed out, most of these schools do not offer a high enough standard of teaching, or even teach the right courses, to reach the next level of schooling.

The authorities show very little interest in improving these conditions. In 1950, only 1·3 per cent of the total budget for Mozambique was allotted to education, and by 1962 this had increased only to 4 per cent. In 1961, the total sum allotted to the missions for African education was $1,050,000.00, whereas some $6 million are collected in annual revenue from the African population. When I visited Mozambique in 1961, I talked to two of the highest officials in the Board of Education: the Director of Education for Mozambique and the Principal of Salazar High School. I asked them about the heavy bias against Africans, and what plans the government had for expanding African education to correct it. The Director of Education told me that nothing could be done to increase the number of African grade school children until more money was made available to expand the whole system. The Principal of Salazar High School evaded my first question on the number of black Africans at secondary schools in Lourenço Marques by simply stating that there were more than at the time when he took up his post. In answer to further questions about their academic performance, he said that the black students compared favourably to the white in the physical sciences and mathematics, but that their performance in the arts, particularly in Portuguese language and literature, was poorer. He also suggested that poor Portuguese might account for their low results in other arts subjects, because although examiners did not know the races of the candidates, they could tell by the poor Portuguese grammar which ones were Africans. Later, talking to a Roman Catholic priest, I again asked about the number of black Africans attending secondary school in Lourenço Marques. He began by proudly pointing out that in Portuguese Africa students are not identified by race, and then went on to make an estimate of twenty. When he noticed my disappoint-ment, he quickly added that there were more African students in the uptown government high school. However, when I visited the school myself, I found that the proportion was still heavily in favour of whites: on talking to some African students, I gathered that there must have been no more than forty black African stu-dents out of an estimated total of 800.

The role of the Church in Mozambique

Since the education of the African is almost entirely in the hands of the Church, it is worth taking a closer look at the whole position of the Church, its activities and attitudes.

While the Colonial Act provides for freedom of conscience and the freedom of the various religions, at the same time and in a contradictory manner it provides for special protection and assistance to the Roman Catholic Church and to its mission programme. Departing from an earlier attitude, held during the first two decades following the establishment of the republic, the Portuguese government recognized the rights and special functions of the Church, which are 'to Christianize and educate, to nationalize and civilize the native populations'. In Mozam-bique this policy is governed by appropriate constitutional

69

provisions, beginning with the Missionary Accord of 1940 – which spelled out in some detail the principles contained in the Concordat of 7 May 1940 between the Vatican and Portugal – and the Missionary Statute of 1941. By these agreements, the Portuguese government is committed to subsidize the Church's missionary programmes, limiting the activities of non-Catholic foreign missionaries and discouraging the influx of Catholic foreign missionaries.

In an estimated Mozambican population of 7,000,000, the number of people who subscribe to the Roman Catholic faith is about 800,000. These are served by about 100 missions and parish churches, led by secular priests and fathers of various orders, including Franciscans, Dominicans, Benedictines, Lazarists, and those of the Holy Ghost Congregation. In 1959 there were in Mozambique 240 priests and fathers. And of these only three priests were Africans. Some of the most important activities of the Catholic Church are 'the founding and directing of schools for Europeans and African children, elementary, secondary and professional schools and seminaries . . . as well as infirmaries and hospitals'. The whole responsibility for educating the African people has been entrusted to the Roman Catholic Church, despite the fact that the overwhelming majority of the Africans are not Christians. And to this has also been attached the responsibility for preparing those Africans who might become assimilated to the Portuguese culture. The Portuguese believe that there is a better chance for an African to become a Portuguese in every respect if he is a Roman Catholic. This belief, often expressed by officials of the government, is well illustrated by a statement made in 1960 by Dr Adriano Moreira, then Under-Secretary of State for Overseas Administration. While emphasizing that political loyalty did not depend upon Christian qualifications, Dr Moreira declared that Catholic missionary activity was inseparably linked to patriotism, and that the formation of Christian qualities led to the formation of Portuguese qualities.

It is this attitude which has led to separating the education of African children from that of the Europeans, a separation which is the more peculiar in that elsewhere in the world, the Catholic

Church insists on educating the children of its members. Yet in Mozambique, the children of the Europeans, who are more than 95 per cent Roman Catholic, are left in the hands of secular schools, run by the State. The intent of this policy is obviously to indoctrinate the children of the native black Mozambicans with Christianity, thereby assuring the government of a population docile and loyal to Portugal.

This attitude of the Portuguese government is so entrenched that it constantly influences policy, even in decisions involving the admission of foreign Christian missionaries, Catholic or Protestant, into the country. Since the seventeenth century, foreign missionaries have been suspected of 'denationalizing the natives', and of acting as advance agents for foreign governments. When these missionaries are Protestant, fears and resentments are multiplied. Consequently, for many years the Protestant missions in Mozambique have been hampered and quite often thwarted by a powerful combination of the Portuguese Catholic clergy and officials of the colonial government. From time to time, public statements are made by high officials of the colonial government attacking Protestant missions, accusing them of fomenting anti-Portuguese sentiments amongst the African population. Lately, indeed, Protestant missionaries have been attacked as responsible for the rise of nationalism in both Angola and Mozambique.

In fact, the leadership of the nationalist movements in the two countries is religiously mixed. In our own Mozambique Liberation Front, most of the members in the Central Committee, which directs the whole programme of the struggle, either are Roman Catholics or come from Catholic families. The man who first directed our military action programme, the late Filipe Magaia, had been baptized in the Roman Catholic Church, as had Samora Machel, the present chief of the Liberation Army. The largest number of our students abroad, who have run away from Portuguese schools either in Mozambique or Portugal, are Roman Catholic. When in May 1961 more than 100 university students from Portuguese colonies in Africa ran away from Portuguese universities to France, Switzerland and West Germany, over eighty of them declared themselves to be either Roman Catholic or to have come from Catholic families. There is, therefore, no evidence to support the Portuguese contention, which must be based rather on the purposes of the Church, its methods and the attitudes which it attempts to inculcate.

The elementary education which the Church provides for Africans is highly religious in content, with a large part of lesson time devoted to religious knowledge. Apart from this, subjects taught are Portuguese, reading, writing and arithmetic, but the standard in all these is very low. The courses are orientated towards Portugal. Such history and geography as are taught are the history and geography of Portugal. Africa is only skimmed in connexion with the Portuguese Empire. Furthermore, a great deal of time is spent on manual work at the expense of academic subjects. Although the proceeds of this work go to the mission, this is not accepted in place of fees. All these features are illustrated by this account of Imbuho mission school by a former pupil, Gabriel Maurício Nantimbo (Cabo Delgado Province):

I studied at the mission, but we weren't well taught. In the first place, they taught us only what they wanted us to learn – the catechism; they didn't want us to learn other things. Then every morning we had to work on the mission land. They said our fathers didn't pay for our food or our school things. The mission also received money from the government, and our families paid them fees. After 1958 our parents even had to buy the hoes with which we cultivated the mission land. (F.I.)

In the course of education, the Church naturally tries to instil moral and political attitudes in its pupils, and in this connexion it is important to examine the role of the Church in relation to the Portuguese State. In general the Portuguese Catholic hierarchy supports the programmes of the Lisbon régime both at home and overseas. And the Vatican does little to alter the relationship. Indeed, on his visit to Portugal in May 1967, the Pope brought a gift of $150,000 to the Portuguese government 'for overseas use', and he nominated the Cardinal of Lisbon to the office of Bishop of the Portuguese Armed Forces, with the rank of brigadier. The attitude of the government to the Church is clearly expressed in a statement made, on 28 August 1967, by the

Under-Secretary for Overseas Administration: 'When the State entrusts the Catholic missions with a share in the work of education, the State is certain that the missions will work for the common good, in the task entrusted to them. And when the Church accepts this task, the Church is equally certain that the State has taken the best path for defending the interests it is its duty to defend. From this we can conclude that, in the auspicious work which, for centuries, they have been accomplishing in Africa, the activities of Church and State will continue in perfect harmony, led by the same ideals.'

For many Portuguese Catholics, being Portuguese and being Catholic are one and the same thing. And we know of no instance during the last forty years when the Roman Catholic Church of Portugal felt compelled to protest officially against the many savage acts of the Portuguese government against the African people. On the contrary, the highest officials of the Church have tended to come out in support of government policy and conduct. The only exception to this rule has been the position of one Church leader in Mozambique, the Bishop of Beira, Monseigneur Sebastião Soares de Resende. For a number of years, he even dared question the government for its treatment of the African cotton growers. In his monthly pastoral letters, published in a Church periodical, he frequently criticized the manner in which the government was carrying out some of its African policies. Bishop Resende is one of the Portuguese liberals who believe in the possibility of creating a new Brazil in Africa, where Portuguese culture can flourish even after independence. The impression one gets of his position, as gleaned from some of his pastorals and a daily newspaper which he is purported to control, is that he can conceive of an independent Mozambique only within a community of Portuguese interests, cultural, religious and economic. His intention was to liberalize the policy rather than to change it radically. But when finally some of his opinions began to annoy the Salazar régime, he was ordered by the Vatican to stop publishing them. Subsequently, the government curtailed some of the privileges which he had previously enjoyed, in particular taking away his responsibilities as director of the only secondary school in Beira.

The clearest statement ever made by a Portuguese Catholic leader of any standing on the question of self-determination and independence has come from Monseigneur Custódio Alvim Pereira, Auxiliary Bishop of Lourenço Marques. If his position is to be taken as representative of the Roman Catholic Church, then the Church is unequivocally against independence. In a recent circular which was read in all Catholic Churches and Seminaries throughout Mozambique, Bishop Pereira outlined ten points intended to convince the clergy that independence for the African people was not only wrong but contrary to the will of God. The statement ran as follows:

1. Independence is irrelevant to the welfare of man. It can be good if the right conditions are present (the cultural conditions do not yet exist in Mozambique).

2. While these conditions are not being produced, to take part in movements for independence is acting against nature.

3. Even if these conditions existed, the Metrópole has the right to oppose independence if the freedoms and rights of man are respected, and if it (the Metrópole) provided for the well-being, the civil and religious progress of all.

4. All the movements which use force (terrorists) are against the natural law, because independence, if it is to be assumed that it is good, must be obtained by peaceful means.

5. When the movement is a terrorist one, the clergy have the obligation, in good conscience, not only to refrain from taking part, but also to oppose it. This [obligation] derives from the nature of his mission [as a religious leader].

6. Even when the movement is peaceful, the clergy must abstain from it in order to have spiritual influence upon all people. The Superior of the Church may impose that abstention; he imposes it now for Lourenço Marques.

7. The native people of Africa have the obligation to thank the colonialists for all the benefits which they receive from them.

8. The educated have the duty to lead those with less education from all the illusions of independence.

9. The present independence movements have, almost all of them, the sign of revolt and of Communism; they have no reason; we must not, therefore, support these movements. The doctrine of the Holy See is quite clear concerning atheistic and revolutionary Communism. The great revolution is that of the Gospel.

10. The Slogan 'Africa for the Africans' is a philosophical monstrosity and a challenge to the Christian civilization, because today's events tell us that it is Communism and Islamism which wish to impose their civilization upon the Africans.

Clearly it is no accident that the Church adopts this approach, and that the education of Africans is entrusted to the Church: it is yet another sign that the aim of Portuguese education for Africans is submission, not development. In theory the aim of education is to help the African become 'civilized' and to make him into a 'Portuguese'. This in itself is a narrow ethnocentric approach, but it would at least offer Africans the opportunity to develop, even if not in the most suitable direction. In practice, however, nothing of the sort is pursued. The system is designed to make it almost impossible for an African to get an education which qualifies him for anything but menial work afterwards. The whole system of African schooling is designed to produce not citizens, but servants of Portugal.

4 The Economics of Exploitation

Portuguese policy places on parallel lines the interests of Europeans as leaders in the transformation of backward regions and the interests of the natives as a mass prepared to become part of a future civilized people. Thus Portugal cannot accept in absolute terms the principle 'paramountcy of native interests', rather on the contrary her traditional methods come closer to what Lugard called 'Dual Mandate'.
Colonizing Traditions, Principles and Methods of the Portuguese, Marcelo Caetano, Lisbon, 1961

The role of the colonies

According to the Portuguese constitution, the government does not accept even a true 'dual mandate' in respect of her colonies: her purpose in holding on to them is first and foremost that she may systematically exploit the resources of the territories, settle Portuguese families in the colonies and regulate the movement of African workers, including the discipline and protection of immigrant workers. All other reasons, such as raising the moral and social standards of the inhabitants and realizing social justice, are stated as secondary.

To understand the economics of this relationship between Portugal and her colonies, one must first consider the economy of Portugal herself. Portugal is small and economically backward. Her territory is a fraction that of Mozambique and her population, at 9 million, is only a little higher than the population of the colony. In 1961 Portugal's total national revenue was 64,200,000 million escudos, which represents a *per capita* income of about $250 a year, one of the lowest in Europe. Her rate of economic growth is slow. She has few mineral resources and little industry. As a result of her mountainous terrain and the primitive methods of agriculture which, practised for centuries, have caused extensive soil erosion, she has a shortage of cultivable land.

Yet despite the shortage of land, half the population is engaged in agriculture, and the situation of these is aggravated by the concentration of land ownership in the hands of a few powerful landlords. Only 0·4 per cent of landowners own 45 per cent of the land, and the 500 biggest landowners control more land than do the 500,000 smallest ones. Unemployment and under-employment are endemic.

The ownership of industry, like that of land is concentrated in the hands of a few capitalists. The average industrial wage is about $1 a day. There has always been a chronic shortage of domestic capital, and the economy is largely supported by foreign investment (until 1930 this was mostly English, but since then Germany, France and America have become important suppliers of capital). The poverty of the population has led to extensive clandestine emigration to France, which the government has tried unsuccessfully to check. The backwardness of the national economy gives Portugal a chronically unfavourable trade balance; her main exports to foreign countries are cork, wolfram, cotton textiles, wines and sardines, while she has to import nearly all the manufactured products, apart from textiles, that she uses. Between 1955 and 1959, the value of her exports covered only 62 per cent of the value of her imports; in 1964 they covered 66 per cent, but since then the gap has increased again.

1964 trade figures*

Imports: 5,257,000 tons worth 22,320 million escudos
Exports: 3,614,000 tons worth 14,831 million escudos

This is partially offset by the trade of the 'overseas provinces', which has always shown a favourable balance of payments with countries other than Portugal and an unfavourable balance of payments with Portugal herself:

* From *Portugal 1967: Any More Questions Please*, Portuguese Information Service.

Under Portugal

1963 distribution of trade of the 'overseas provinces'* (in millions of escudos)

	Imports	Exports
Total trade	11,370	9,888
With Portugal	4,219	3,193
With the OECD countries	3,628	4,650
With the USA	646	1,712

Recent trade figures for Mozambique show that during the first six months of 1967, she had a negative balance of 668 million escudos within the escudo zone and a favourable balance of 343 million escudos with the rest of the world.

Already one can see why the colonies are important to Portugal: their resources can compensate for Portugal's own lack; they provide for a mass of poverty-stricken and frequently unemployed people an emigration outlet which, at the same time, keeps them within the jurisdiction of Portugal, contributing to the national income and liable for military service; since the colonies have a favourable trade balance with countries other than Portugal, they help her to retain reserves of foreign exchange. An examination of the economic structure will show in greater detail how Portugal takes advantage of these assets.

The principles underlying the economic system in metropolitan Portugal are entrenched in the basic laws governing the corporative organization of the State. For example, it is stated in the constitution of the State that 'private enterprise is recognized as the most prolific instrument of progress and of the economy of the nation'; the State is relegated to coordinator and regulator of the economic and social life, and arbitrator of the economic and social goals. The constitution, indeed, prohibits the State from engaging in trade or establishing any industries, except where private economic interests cannot afford the initial investment costs. Since the real political power in Portugal resides in the *corporative chamber*, a body composed of representatives of guilds (*grémios*), 'the economic interests of the nation' are actually determined by a powerful few.

This same system is extended to cover the overseas territories.

* From *Portugal 1967: Any More Questions Please*, Portuguese Information Service.

In the constitution of Portugal, the economic relationship with the overseas territories is defined as follows:

The economic organization of the Portuguese overseas territories shall form part of the general economic organization of the Portuguese Nation and shall thereby take its place in the world economy.

Within this structure, it is also envisaged that metropolitan Portugal will 'secure, through measures taken by the competent bodies, a proper balance of the various economic interests'. As in metropolitan Portugal, guilds have been established in Mozambique, for producers of cereals, vegetable oil processing industries, tea and tobacco growers, whose role is to help the government in planning and directing the exploitation of the country's natural and human resources.

Prime Minister Salazar has himself stated that the overseas territories were 'a logical solution to Portugal's problem of over-population, to settle Portuguese nationals in the colonies and for the colonies to produce raw materials to sell to the motherland in exchange for manufactured goods.'

Although foreign interests in Portugal herself work under special legal restrictions, in the overseas territories they do not apply. Usually the Portuguese government requires the participation of Portuguese capital in foreign-owned companies, the registration of companies, and the appointment of Portuguese nationals to the boards of directors, although the Portuguese capital need not exceed 50 per cent. The only sector of the economy in which 51 per cent of the capital must be Portuguese is that concerned with the use and exploitation of land concessions. This requirement, however, was not made applicable to overseas territories until 1947. In Mozambique nearly all the foreign companies holding large tracts of land came into existence long before this, and to date Portuguese participation is insignificant.

Even the 1947 decree introducing the 51 per cent Portuguese participation requirement for overseas territories was not made binding, since the same law empowered the Minister for Overseas Territories to waive the requirement in 'special cases'. Furthermore, the restrictions which were originally imposed on foreign investments were removed in April 1951, and new regulations adopted whereby enterprises entirely or largely foreign-owned might be established in the various economic sectors of the overseas territories, with the same rights of duty and exemption as national enterprises so long as they were owned by residents of a Portuguese territory or persons domiciled in overseas territories.

Then, faced with colonial wars since the 1961 outbreak in Angola, the government decided to eliminate all restrictions on the entry of foreign capital to the colonies, in the hope of gaining financial and political support abroad for the maintenance of the Portuguese Empire.

As part of the policy of exploiting the resources of the colonial territories, the Salazar régime insists on a process of economic integration, establishing rules in 1961 whereby the parent country and overseas territories must within ten years become one single economic community – commercial and monetary. This means that by the end of 1971, the existing quantitative customs restrictions between the colonies and the parent country will have been progressively eliminated. According to the terms of this law, all foreign exchange earned by the overseas territories in payment for their exports must be directly deposited with the Bank of Portugal in Lisbon, which in its turn will credit to the respective colony the corresponding amount in Portuguese currency. In order to enable each colony to pay its inter-territorial debts, Portugal created a *monetary fund* of the *escudo zone*.

In pursuit of her economic aims, it was, in short, necessary to: (1) integrate the whole economy of the country with that of the colonies; (2) centralize in Lisbon the political machinery of the colonial empire; and (3) bar all tendencies towards independence in her African possessions, to the point of establishing an army much beyond her internal needs.

In order to facilitate control of the economic life of the colonies as well as for political reasons, the Portuguese government decided unilaterally to alter the constitution in 1951, declaring Portugal to be one nation embracing not only metropolitan Portugal, but also all her overseas territories. Prior to this, the Salazar régime had gradually reduced and finally eliminated any financial contributions from Portugal to the development of the colonies, by insisting that each colony must pay its own expenses with its own resources: that (1) the budgets of the overseas territories be balanced; (2) the receipts come from local resources; and (3) the expenses be completely met by the budget of the territory.

Furthermore, colonial territories are obliged to pay for the cost of maintaining a number of political, economic and educational institutions in metropolitan Portugal, such as the Council of Overseas Provinces, the General Overseas Agency, the Institute of Tropical Medicine and the Centre for Overseas Studies. In 1961, such extra-territorial expenses cost the three African colonies more than 35 million escudos. And the Portuguese government insists that all but one-third of the budget for the non-governmental organizations, such as the boards for co-ordinating the exports of cotton, cereals and coffee, be borne by the overseas territories.

Despite these measures, however, it would appear that Portugal enjoys a net economic gain only from Angola, and that in the case of Mozambique she actually loses financially. This does not mean, however, that in terms of real economic gain she is the loser. The paradox lies in the details of economic intercourse between Mozambique and metropolitan Portugal. Mozambique is principally an exporter of raw materials and an importer of manufactured goods. With the exception of vegetable oils, meat and fish canning, there are at present no local manufacturing industries of any importance. Most of the sugar grown is exported raw to be refined in metropolitan Portugal. The same applies to cotton; it is sent to Portugal, for the textile industries there to convert it into thread and cloth. Since 1961 this pattern has begun to change, and with the help of foreign capital a number of small factories and assembly plants have been established in the colony. Recently, even some cotton industries were allowed to start producing textiles in Mozambique, since better cotton from elsewhere (like the United States) is now available at competitive prices. In spite of this, the Portuguese textile industries still prefer to buy most of their cotton requirements from Mozambique and Angola, for three reasons: they are able to pay in national currency; prices are fixed by the government, sufficiently below those of the world market to represent a considerable saving; and they have a captive 12 million people to consume their finished goods. Recently Professor Quitanilha, chief of Mozambique's Cotton Research Centre, said that if Portugal had had to purchase abroad all the cotton that her textile industry had consumed in the past few years, this would have meant an annual expenditure of some £12 million. Instead, the actual annual income that the cotton industry brings to the Portuguese economy is £18 million.

Looking over the annual import list of manufactured goods for Mozambique, one notices that there is a preponderance of two important items, *cotton textiles* and *wines and spirits*, both produced in Portugal in large quantities. Indeed, Mozambique imports more cloth and wines and spirits (both in quantity and value) than she does industrial and farm equipment. Of goods which have to be imported from outside the escudo zone, it is worth noting the large numbers of private vehicles in Mozambique, which are obviously not for the consumption of the poor African population, but for the privileged few non-Africans.

Thus the structure of exchange between Portugal and the overseas territories is typical of the Portuguese colonial system, in that the economic life of the colonial territories is geared towards serving the interests of metropolitan Portugal rather than their own; the overseas territories supply metropolitan Portugal with tropical products, basic raw materials, while serving as a captive market and a dumping ground for cheap industrial goods, and the wines and spirits for which Portugal is famed. Recently, too, they have acquired a new importance as a means of earning hard currency. Methods of production in Mozambique reflect this scale of priorities: Portugal's interests are put before Mozambique's, as within Mozambique the interests of the white minority are put before those of Mozambican Africans.

To promote such a policy, the Salazar régime, right from its inception, set out to increase the production of commercial agricultural produce by introducing new methods of land distribution and control; and by forcibly reducing the production of agricultural consumer goods traditionally used by the African population. It also discouraged the development of African agricultural and consumer cooperatives for fear that they might compete with European settler interests.

Production of cash crops

Mozambique is at the moment primarily an agricultural country, and the most important of her products are: cotton, sisal, cane sugar, rice, tea, tobacco, copra, cashew nuts, ground nuts and various types of oil seed. Production of these in the territory follows a certain racial pattern which illustrates the colonial economic policy and practice of Portugal. In general, cotton and rice are produced by Africans, on individual or family plots. Copra, sugar cane, tea and sisal are produced by European farmers, principally on large individual farms, or on estates and plantations, which require much initial capital.

The production of rice and cotton by African farmers is not spontaneous; because of controlled prices, there is no profit incentive which might make them undertake it of their own accord. The government compels them to raise such crops, sometimes on specially allotted plots of land, sometimes on their own traditional holdings.

Let us take the production of cotton as an example. When Salazar first came to power in 1928, the Portuguese colonies in Africa produced about 800 tons of cotton, while the Portuguese textile industries needed 17,000 tons. One of the first steps taken by the Salazar régime was to institute a system of forced cotton cultivation in the two main African colonies. In Angola, special legal decrees made it obligatory for all able-bodied Africans living in designated areas to grow cotton. In Mozambique, no further legal initiative was necessary, since the obligation to produce cotton could be derived from earlier general legal provisions for African labour and farming. By the middle 1950s, the number of Africans engaged in the cultivation of cotton had risen to half a million, and production in Mozambique alone had reached 140,000 tons. The Portuguese textile industry, which employs a third of Portugal's industrial labour force and accounts for a fifth of the value of total exports, took 82 per cent of its raw materials from the colonies.

Up to 1961, the direction and supervision of cotton production belonged to the agents of the concessionary companies, supported by the local administrative services, under the overall guidance of the Cotton Export Board. Under this system, the Board designated the areas where cotton was to be grown, determining the amount of land to be cultivated by each African individual or family in the cotton zone.

In 1930, the Cotton Export Board drew up 'general instructions', which were later approved by the Governor-General, setting out the procedure for cotton growing by Africans. All able-bodied African males between the ages of eighteen and fifty-five were to be designated as 'cotton farmers', and were expected to cultivate at least 2·5 acres of cotton each, plus 1·5 acres for each wife after the first, plus an equal area of food crops. Single women between the ages of eighteen and forty-five, and men between fifty-six and sixty, were designated 'cotton cultivators', responsible for 1·5 acres of cotton, plus an equal area of food crops.

The further organization was outlined by Professor Marvin Harris in his monograph *Portugal's African Wards*:*

In this modern serfdom, the role of the medieval lord is exercised by twelve Portuguese companies, each of which has received monopolistic concession rights over cotton production in vast areas of Mozambique. *Indigenas* within the concession areas of each company are assigned cotton acreage by the administrative authorities. They have no choice in the matter and must plant, cultivate and harvest cotton wherever they are told. Then they must sell the raw cotton to the concession company of their area at prices which are fixed by the government far below those available on the international market. . . . In 1956, there were 519,000 African cultivators participating in the cotton campaign . . . the actual number of men, women and children being forced to plant cotton (on acreage taken out of food production) probably exceeds one million. In 1956, the 519,000 sellers received an average of $11·17 per person as their family's reward for an entire year of work.

It was the duty of the Portuguese administration to ensure that all the cotton produced each year was presented at the market places for the concessionary company to buy, so that the African producer might not sell his cotton elsewhere. In this way both the private company, enjoying monopoly rights, and the Portuguese government were able to set the price at will, thus assuring themselves of the profit that they wanted for the year.

* New York, 1958.

This system may well have enriched the European companies involved but it has had a different and often disastrous effect on a large proportion of the Africans. It has disrupted their normal economic activities, reducing the output of consumer food crops and causing recurrent famines; while during the planting, cultivating and harvesting periods, the average African has been under constant persecution by the police, busily combing every house, and driving out every man, woman and child to the cotton fields every day, in order to make certain that they do nothing else but work in cotton. Furthermore, the eagerness of the concessionary companies to make yet greater profits has induced the government to force Africans into growing cotton on marginal lands, resulting in untold economic hardships to the cultivators themselves, most of whom earn less than £2 10s. a year from the sale of cotton.

The 1961 'reforms' made some changes in the system, the chief of which was to remove the legal basis for compulsory cultivation. As in other fields, however, the change in the law had little effect in practice. The essential characteristics of the system remain as they were before 1961. The following accounts, which illustrate this, are by Mozambicans who were working in cotton producing areas at least till 1964, when the liberation struggle forced some of the companies to close down. The conditions they describe are prevalent today in those regions not yet deeply affected by the war.

Rita Mulumbua (Niassa Province): My parents are peasants. On our land we grew cassava, beans and maize. We also grew cotton which we sold to a company. We sold a bag of cotton for from 25 escudos (90 cents) to 50 escudos ($1,80 cents) depending on the quality and the year. In a good year my father must have sold 10 bags. He paid 195 escudos ($7·0) tax.

I worked in the fields growing cotton. We didn't want cotton, but we had to grow it; we wanted to grow cassava, beans and maize. If we refused to grow cotton, they arrested us, put us in chains, beat us and then sent us away to a place from where one often didn't come back. When I was a child I knew Chief Navativa; they arrested him and he hasn't been seen since. (F.I.)

Gabriel Mauricio Nantimbo (Cabo Delgado Province): My whole

family produced cotton for the *Companhia Agrícola Algodoeira*. When the company came to exploit our region, everyone was forced to cultivate one field of cotton. Each person was given seed. Then one had to clear the field, thin the cotton, because when there are too many plants the cotton does not grow well, and then remove the weeds. Finally, after the harvest, the company told us where to take the cotton and then bought it from us. They paid us very badly for it. It was extremely difficult to make a living because we were badly paid for it, and we didn't have time to look after our other crops: cotton needs constant attention; you have to keep weeding the field and thinning out the plants.

The time of cotton growing was a time of great poverty, because we could only produce cotton; we got a poor price for it, and we did not have time to grow other crops. We were forced to produce cotton. The people didn't want to: they knew cotton is the mother of poverty, but the company was protected by the government. We knew that anyone who refused to grow it would be sent to the plantations on São Tomé where he would work without any pay at all. So as not to make our poverty any greater, then; so as not to leave the family and leave the children to suffer alone, we had to grow cotton. The company and government work together closely to enforce the system. . . . One day my uncle fell sick and could not look after (his) field. The company manager sent him to the authorities, and he told them he was sick. . . . The administrator said to him: 'You're a bad man. Do you think others don't fall sick? Is everyone who works in the fields in good health?' My uncle replied, 'There are different sorts of illness. With some you can go on working, with others you can't. I couldn't work.' They arrested him and sent him to São Tomé for a year. (F.I.)

European producers of cotton and other cash crops are not subject to the same regulations as the Africans. Aside from the fact that they receive large tracts of land from the government, they are favoured by the banks for loans. Above all, they are not obliged to sell their produce to the concessionary companies, but can put it on the open market, governed by standard world prices. The sums paid to African producers and quoted by Rita Mulumbua are well below world prices, which makes possible the low resale price to the Portuguese textile producers: recently cotton was being sold to the Portuguese industry at 17 escudos per kilogram, while in the rest of the world the standard price was 20–25 escudos.

Government legislation recognizes only Europeans as producers, with the right to be registered on the export boards, although in practice most of the work is done by African labour, either in paid employment on plantations or as principal growers themselves.

The production of other cash crops, apart from rice, takes place mostly on large plantations, where the labour force is African but the responsibility for production rests with the management. In other respects the system is similar: there is the same cooperation between company and government; there is the same element of compulsion and of low costs for the company, in this instance provided by paying low wages to the African instead of low prices for his products. A description of work on a tea plantation in Zambézia shows that the effect on the African population is very much the same:

Joaquim Maquival (Zambézia Province): We had to work on the government land, at least it isn't government land; it belongs to a company but it was the government which made us work on it. It was the land of the *Sociedade de Chá Oriental de Milange*. The government came and arrested us in our villages and sent us to the company; that is, the company paid money to the administration or the government, and then the government arrested us and gave us to the company. I began working for the company when I was twelve; they paid me fifteen escudos a month (53 cents). I worked from six in the morning until twelve noon, when we stopped for two hours; then again from two p.m. until six p.m. The whole family worked for the company; my brothers, my father – my father is still there. My father earned and still earns 150 escudos a month ($5.3). He had to pay 195 escudos tax yearly. We didn't want to work for the company, but if we refused the government sent the police to the villages, and they arrested those who refused, and if they ran away the government circulated photographs and a hunt was started. When they caught them they beat them and put them in prison, and when they came out of prison they had to go and work but without pay; they said that as they ran away they didn't need the money. . . . Thus in our own fields only our mothers were left who could not do much. All we had to eat was the little our mothers were able to grow. We had neither sugar nor tea – we had to work on the tea but we didn't know what it tasted like. Tea never came to our homes. (F.I.)

Mixed farming

The normal occupation of most Africans, if not disturbed, would be subsistence farming. But when the government does not actively hinder them, it does little to help. African farmers are entitled to very little support and aid from the government, apart from the occasional distribution of quality seeds, which has to be repaid in kind anyway. On the contrary, they are faced with all sorts of legal and administrative obstacles before they can qualify as independent farmers at all.

Since 1928, when the Salazar régime was first established, the government has issued a number of decrees restricting the freedom of Africans to choose where to work. From 1928 to 1961, an African could engage in independent farming only under the following conditions:

1. He must cultivate permanently one or more plots, which had to conform with official requirements for land cultivation.

2. He must be the main and permanent agent of the various activities in connexion with his holding, where he might have the help of his relations and paid employees or exchange service with other workers.

3. He must reside with his family on one of his plots.

4. He must have paid all his taxes.

5. He must maintain his activities in accordance with the instructions of the Governor-General.

The above requirements are so difficult to fulfil that only a few people can qualify as independent farmers. And as if these were not sufficient to discourage Africans from venturing into independent farming, the Portuguese government has decreed further that an African farmer can be expelled from his land if, among other things:

1. He has been away and not taking care of his plot for more than a total of four months in a year;

2. after three years, he has not shown that he was achieving adequate agricultural development, as evident from the growth and increased value of his cultivated areas and livestock;

3. he has not, within three years, built a brick house on his plots or close to them.

Even the ordinary peasant who is not trying to establish himself as an independent farmer faces many difficulties. The most persistent is head tax. In order to pay this, most peasants have to produce some crop for sale; but, again, prices paid to African producers are very low. For example, in one area peasants were paid 1 escudo (about 3 cents) a kilogram for peanuts by local traders who sold them again at 5 escudos.

The other common threat is land alienation. In theory, traditional lands, as differentiated from land under white settlement, belong to the Africans. Article 38 of the 1955 Native Statute for Mozambique and Angola reaffirmed this policy:

Natives who live in tribal organizations are guaranteed ... the use and development, for their crops, and for the pasture of their cattle.

But under the heavy pressure of European settlers, the Portuguese government yielded. Some of the native land was expropriated, often without compensation, and given over to large plantations of sugar cane, tea, or sisal, and for the settlement of white immigrants from Portugal. For this again, we have direct testimony from the people affected:

Natacha Deolinda (Manica and Sofala Province): At Buzi (Beira) the Portuguese bought all the land. There were some villages on the land, and the people in them were driven out and had to leave their homes, their land, and look for another place to live. They received no compensation for their houses; they were just driven out. In our area we were forced to leave, abandoning our fields, and the Portuguese planted sugar cane everywhere. We were not allowed to use the wells we had dug; all the water was reserved for the cane. If one of us was found with some sugar cane, they arrested us and made us pay fifty escudos for a tiny piece of it. They said we had stolen it, and if we didn't have any money the administration made us work for a week in the plantation, supposedly to pay for the bit of sugar cane. (F.I.)

In areas where the land was taken not for development as a plantation, but to settle white peasant farmers, a few of the original African owners were allowed to remain. This brings us to another of the many contradictions in Portuguese-ruled Mozambique: the establishment of the so-called 'multi-racial settlements', in the rich river valleys of the Limpopo, Incomati and Zambezi basins, known in Portuguese as *colonatos*. The system was dreamed up by Salazar's sociologists, who claimed that any attempt to advance from a traditional African way of life to a modern industrial society in a short period of time would not be feasible. Instead, they suggested that the best course to follow would be the establishment of an agrarian society through the settlement of Portuguese peasants in government colonization projects, in some of which the African was to take part, and through the development of African agricultural colonies which would make possible favourable conditions for the economic and spiritual assimilation of the African. Part of the motivation for this scheme was to help expedite the increase of the Portuguese population in Mozambique. But the officially stated aim was to create a semi-literate population of Africans and Portuguese holding rural Portuguese values, dedicated to the land and politically conservative, so as to absorb and divert the energies of the rising African, and render him unable to threaten the large European economic interests represented by the agricultural estates, the main economic props of the colony.

The first serious attempts at establishing such settlements took place in the early 1950s, and the best known *colonatos* in Mozambique are to be found in the southern districts, especially in the Limpopo Valley. While there are a few African farmers in these agricultural settlements, the overwhelming majority are white Portuguese immigrants.

While visiting Mozambique in 1961, I talked to some farmers who were members of government-sponsored cooperatives in Zavala, Chibuto and Chai-Chai. I also visited some new agricultural projects in the Manjacaze area, organized on the model of the Israeli *kibbutzim*. The prevailing complaint among the African members was that the government did not allow them to bargain with the outside purchasers of their produce. In other words, the cooperatives were being used as another cheap way of supplying agricultural goods to the great concessionary companies at the expense of the African farmer.

There are some Portuguese and foreign economists who are impressed by the few cooperatives now operating in the southern districts of Mozambique. They believe that these institutions point the way to the future, and that the self-administration and 'democratic' rule learned in the cooperatives may be an important first step in moving away from the paternalistic government of the Portuguese colonies. Let us assume that there is some small truth in this point of view; yet in 1960, there were only 12,000 farmers participating in cooperative projects, out of an estimated population of over 6,500,000, or one-twentieth of 1 per cent of the total population.

Labour

We have already seen how, from the early stages of their control, the Portuguese regarded the African labour force as one of the colonial resources to be exploited for the benefit of Portugal. We outlined the labour laws, and indicated how the production of cash crops was based on the underpaid forced labour permitted by such laws. It is worth-while here to summarize the main methods of labour exploitation and their place in the overall economy of the colony.

Six main types of labour can be distinguished:

1. *Correctional labour*, imposed instead of a prison sentence, following conviction for infringement of the Criminal Code, or indirectly for an infringement of the Labour Code or for non-payment of tax. Since the modification made to the law in 1960–62, conviction in the latter cases is for contempt of court, following on non-compliance with a court order to pay a tax or compensation fee. This type of labour is generally completely unpaid.

2. *Obligatory labour*, originally based on a government circular of 5 May 1947, ordering all 'natives' to work six months of the year for the State, a company or an individual. Since 1961 this has been abolished; but, by ministerial edict, labour can be called on to redress economic ills (9 May 1961, no. 24), and based on this, the practice of 'obligatory labour' continues. This sort of labour is usually paid at very low rates (2 or 3 escudos a day). It was intended in the main for road building and similar public works, but unofficially is often drafted into plantations.

3. *Contract labour*, regulated under the present rural labour code, and called contract because the relationship between employer and employee, as set out in the code, is of the contract type. A failure by the employee to fulfil his obligation can be punished with various civil sanctions, which may lead to a criminal conviction and a sentence to correctional labour. Contract labour is also paid at low rates.

4. *Voluntary labour*, where an individual employee is engaged directly by an employer. This is the case mostly with domestic work, and is found rarely outside the towns.

5. *Forced cultivation*, where the worker is paid not for his labour but for the product of it.

6. *Export labour*, or labour sent abroad, mainly to South Africa, in return for various payments to the Portuguese government.

This last type of labour is the only one whose workings have not already been described. In its present form it is based on an agreement between the Portuguese and South African governments, dating from 11 September 1928 and carrying the ponderous title: 'Agreement on the Emigration of Natives from Mozambique to the Transvaal; Questions Relating to the Railways and Commercial Relations Between the Colony of Mozambique and South Africa.' It allowed for the recruitment of at least 65,000 and at most 100,000 Mozambicans by the Transvaal mining corporation. The Witwatersrand Native Labour Association, already favoured in the earlier agreement of 1903, was given charge of recruitment and required to pay an amount of £2 16s. per head to the Mozambican colonial government for every man recruited to serve a period of eighteen months. The agreement also specified that, except for a small advance, the wages of the Mozambicans were to be paid to the government, which would hand it over only on the return of the recruits, after deducting tax and in Portuguese currency. The South African government also agreed to use the Port of Lourenço Marques for 47·5 per cent of the exports from and imports to the Transvaal. A similar agreement was signed with Southern Rhodesia, although the demand for Mozambican labour was much smaller there.

The export of labour remains an extremely important aspect of the Mozambican economy. In 1960 there were more than 400,000 Mozambican workers in South Africa and Southern Rhodesia, providing one of the colony's main sources of revenue and foreign exchange. The budget in 1961 allowed for a total receipt of 6,300,000 million escudos (90,000 million pounds); and of this sum, the export of labour was expected to account for 1,200,000 million.

Of the six types of labour described above, the first five are designed to produce profits for companies and thus indirectly for the government by providing very low cost production; the last is designed to produce revenue and foreign exchange for the government directly.

Mineral resources and industry

Before the Portuguese came to East Africa, some gold and silver were exported from the area now occupied by Mozambique and Southern Rhodesia. The early Portuguese adventurers dreamt of finding a great store of such precious metals in the interior, but their expectations were not fulfilled. Until well into this century, prospecting revealed little of any value, and the colony refused to yield anything but the modest profits to be made from agricultural exploitation. Recently, though, the situation has been dramatically changed by the discovery of several important minerals, including coal, bauxite, asbestos, tantalum and niobium, modest quantities of gold and copper, and reservoirs of oil and natural gas.

The realization that there might be important mineral resources in Mozambique came at about the same time that the Portuguese government found itself forced to relax restrictions on foreign investment in the 'overseas provinces'. These two factors combined to encourage a massive influx of foreign capital into Mozambique from the early 1960s.

This heavy participation of foreign capital is by no means a new phenomenon, as even the first 'big three' concession companies were largely financed from abroad. The difference lies in the new type of investment and in its origins. Earlier investment was confined mainly to agricultural schemes, and the main

93

source of capital was Britain. The Sena Sugar Estates is one of the most important companies dating from this phase of investment. It is largely British owned and is the biggest sugar producer in all the Portuguese colonies: between 1965 and 1966, it accounted for 70 per cent of total output; it employs 25,000 African workers, and in 1967 showed a profit of £1,400,000 before tax.

The new phase of investment, on the other hand, has been dominated by South Africa and the United States, although Britain, France and Japan have also been important, and smaller Western European countries, such as Belgium, Sweden and Switzerland, have contributed. The extraction of minerals, and small processing and manufacturing industries, have taken precedence over agricultural production. The search for oil has taken a particularly prominent place: American owned Gulf Oil started prospecting as early as 1953 and was granted concession rights in 1958, since extended several times. The company has made a number of successful strikes in Southern Mozambique including the discovery of natural gas at Pande, but the extent of the reserves is still a matter for speculation. Another American company which has been prospecting for several years now is the Pan American International Oil Corporation. In 1967 both companies were granted further concessions. Gulf made another natural gas strike, near the Buzi river, about 30 miles from the deposit at Pande. The total gas deposits in this region are at present estimated at some 3,000 million cubic metres.

Also in 1967 prospecting rights were granted to three new American companies – Sunray Mozambique Oil Company, Clark Mozambique Oil Company, and Skelly Mozambique Oil Company – and a group of South African and French companies. The concession is granted initially for three years, during which the minimum expenditure must be 11 million escudos in the first year, 35 million in the second, and 56 million in the third. The companies will pay 3 million escudos in surface rent during the first three years, and on renewal of the concession, 200 escudos per square kilometre.

The French and South African group consists of the Anglo American Corporation of South Africa, the Société Nationale des Pétroles d'Aquitaine, and Entreprises de Recherche et d'Activités

Petrolière. Their concession covers a total area of 14,000 square miles, including an off-shore region. Investment during the first three years is to be 140 million escudos.

In the last two years, the discovery of metal deposits has also been attracting foreign funds. In 1967 a large deposit of high grade iron ore was found near Porto Amélia, and the rights to exploit it have been granted to the Japanese group, Sumitomo, which will invest 50 million US dollars in the project and plans a special rail link to Nacala. The ore has a 60 per cent iron content, and reserves are estimated at 360 million tons. Production is expected to reach 5 million tons in the first year. To process part of this ore, two blast furnaces are being built at Beira jointly by the Sociedade Algodoeira de Fomento and the Sher Company of Rhodesia.

Other recent discoveries include a deposit of tantalite in Moçambique district; deposits of copper ore, azurite and malachite near Nacala; gold near Vila Manica; and a new vein of diamonds at Catuane on the South African border.

In manufacturing, investment has been directed mainly towards processing plants for agricultural products or assembly plants for imported manufactured goods. Typical are the South African sugar mill being built near Beira, the Nestlé milk processing plant in Lourenço Marques and the American Firestone tyre factory in Beira. More recent plans include the processing of bauxite, the manufacture of ammonia and of chemical fertilizer. Four companies – the South African firm, Frazer and Chalmers; the French firms, Sodeix and Socaltra; and the Portuguese Sociedad Química Geral de Moçambique – are involved in a project to build a chemical fertilizer plant near Lourenço Marques, which will have a capacity of 170,000 tons and will require an investment of 250,000,000 escudos.

All these developments in extracting and manufacturing industry are bringing into Mozambique large supplies of foreign capital and will certainly increase the total national income of the country. The economic expansion attributed to these investments is, however, extremely superficial; it is not making, and even in the long run is not likely to make, much impression on the extremely low overall standard of living in the country. For, essentially, the nature of the projects has been dictated by the interests of the investors and of the Portuguese government, not by the needs of Mozambique. There are three important factors which prevent this type of development from providing the majority of the population with any significant benefits.

First of all, because most of the new factories are sited in either of the two major urban centres, Beira and Lourenço Marques, any improvement in wages and industrial conditions which might result from their presence (no significant improvement is yet evident) would be extremely localized in its effects. Less than 4 per cent of Africans live in these two towns, and even the present rate of industrialization is only just sufficient to absorb the present gradual increase in the urban labour force. Growing prosperity in these towns might affect the immediate rural hinterland; but in a vast country like Mozambique, with its poor network of communications, it will do nothing to improve conditions for the great majority of the rural population. The oil extraction industry, although situated in the country and scattered over a wide area, can also not directly benefit much of the population because it essentially requires very little local labour.

The second factor relates to the use of revenue from new industry. It can be argued that concentrated high-capital, low-labour demanding industry will still benefit the whole country through the increased income made available to the government. In Mozambique, however, the government's share of revenue is not being channelled into the much needed social services, but into the war: in 1967 Mozambique's share of support for the Portuguese armed forces was set at 838,000,000 escudos, to be obtained from local revenue. In order to cover this, government expenditure elsewhere had to be cut. Thus, while in 1967 expenditure on defence rose by 20 per cent, allocations for agriculture and forestry were reduced by 30 per cent, and allocations for public works by 50 per cent.*

Thirdly, in several instances the government is granting such favourable terms to attract the investment that it is sacrificing much of its potential revenue, allowing long tax-free working periods and the wholesale export of profits. In 1963, for instance,

* United Nations General Assembly, 23rd session, A/7200/add.3.

when a joint South African–Portuguese chamber of commerce was set up in Johannesburg to finance development in Mozambique, the Governor-General agreed, among other things, to grant a ten-year tax-free working period to foreign enterprises. In 1967 a report by the South African Handelsinstitut stressed the need for guarantees on the repatriation of capital and earnings, and recommended tax advantages for new industries. The investment terms being granted are often so favourable to the investor, and offer the administration in Mozambique so little financial gain, that it seems clear that the concessions to foreign capital are aimed more at securing political advantages than at opening the way to real economic progress.

Cabora Bassa and the Zambezi Valley

The Zambezi Valley scheme is the king-pin of Portugal's plans for development in Mozambique. The Zambezi Valley itself is already one of the richest agricultural areas, and recently a number of important minerals have been discovered there. In 1962 *Diário de Lisboa* announced that plans were afoot for the extraction of titanium, magnetite and fluor. Coal and iron were already being mined in modest quantities, but it was estimated that the export of iron alone could bring in an annual total of £25 million. The most important aspect of the plan, however, is the construction of a giant dam at Cabora Bassa. This is envisaged as a joint project with South Africa, and there will be considerable backing from Western Europe and the United States.

Five international groups competed for the tender to build the dam, and in July 1968 it was awarded to Zamco, a consortium organized by the Anglo American Corporation of South Africa with the participation of French, West German and Swedish firms. Financial backing is being provided by the Banque de Paris et Pays Bas, Union Acceptances of Johannesburg, the Deutsche Bank, and the Banca Comercial Italiana. Some associated projects will also be backed by the Bank of America and Portuguese banks.

The dam will be the largest in Africa, will flood an area of

1,000 square miles, and will produce 17 billion kilowatt hours of hydro-electric power, to serve a radius of 900 miles. It is scheduled to be completed by 1974, and the estimated cost will be £130 million.

This great scheme is in line with the other recent commercial projects in Mozambique; little of the wealth it could create will, under the present arrangement, filter down to the African population of Mozambique. The Zambezi valley is already an area of settlers, where a large amount of land is held by white farmers or plantation owners, and where the Portuguese have announced plans for the settlement of 1 million more Portuguese immigrants along the river. (Considering that the total population of Portugal is about 9 million, this figure can be taken at all seriously only if moves to settle large numbers of non-Portuguese whites are assumed as well.) In 1967 the Mozambique Cotton Institute announced definite plans to settle 3,250 families in the Zambezi valley, and 231 families had already established themselves within a year of the plans having been publicized. During the building of the dam, employment preference will be given to Portuguese soldiers who have completed their service in Mozambique. No doubt, part of the idea behind this last arrangement is that they should also help police the area and protect the site against nationalist action.

The main beneficiary of the plan will be not Mozambique, however, but South Africa. Dr Mário Ferreira, secretary general of Zamco and a director of Anglo American, has stated that South Africa will be the largest consumer of power. A transmission line is planned to link Cabora Bassa with Johannesburg, 870 miles away. Dr Ferreira added that the cost of the power would be among the lowest in the world. Rhodesia and Malawi will also absorb some of the power.

Portugal's cut from this project is clearly political rather than economic. The plan draws South Africa closer to Portugal and gives her an important stake in the future of Mozambique.

Part Two : Towards Independence

5 Resistance – The Search for a National Movement

And ask no more
to know what I am
I'm nothing but a lump of flesh
in which, its cry swollen great with hope
the revolt of Africa has merged.
From 'If you want to know who I am', by Noémia de Sousa

Like all African nationalism, the Mozambican form was born out of the experience of European colonialism. The source of national unity is the common suffering during the last fifty years spent under effective Portuguese rule. The nationalist assertion did not rise out of a stable community, in history a linguistic, territorial, economic and cultural unity. In Mozambique, it was colonial domination which produced the territorial community and created the basis for a psychological coherence, founded on the experience of discrimination, exploitation, forced labour, and other such aspects of colonial rule.

Communication, however, has been limited between the separate communities subjected to these same experiences. All forms of communication previously came from above, through the medium of the colonial administration. And this naturally slowed down the development of a single consciousness throughout the territorial area. In Mozambique, the situation has been aggravated by the 'Greater Portugal' policy, whereby the colony is referred to as a 'province' of Portugal, the people called 'Portuguese' by the authorities. On the radio, in the newspapers, in the schools, there is a great deal of talk about 'Portugal', and very little about 'Mozambique'. Among the peasantry, such propaganda has done a great deal to hinder the development of a 'Mozambique' concept; and as Portugal is too distant an idea to provide a unifying factor, this has also fostered tribalism by not helping people to look beyond their immediate social unit.

In many areas where the population is small and widely scattered, contact between the colonial power and the people has been so superficial that little personal experience of domination existed. There were some groups in Eastern Niassa who had never seen the Portuguese before the outbreak of the present war. In such areas the people had little sense of belonging either to a nation or a colony, and it was at first hard for them to understand the struggle. The arrival of the Portuguese army, however, very rapidly changed this.

Popular resistance

Wherever the presence of the colonizing power was felt, some kind of resistance was shown, taking various forms from armed insurrection to wholesale exodus. But at any given moment, it was only a limited community, small in relation to the whole society, which rose against the colonizer, while the opposition itself was limited because directed against only one aspect of domination, the concrete aspect which affected that particular community at that particular time.

Active resistance was finally crushed in 1918, with the defeat of the Mokombe (King) of Barwe, in the Tete region. And from the early 1930s, the colonial administration of the young fascist state spread across Mozambique, destroying, often physically, the traditional power structure.

From this time on, both repression and resistance hardened. But the centre of resistance shifted from the traditional hierarchies, which became docile puppets of the Portuguese, to individuals and groups – though for long these remained as isolated in their aims and their activities as the traditional leaders had been.

A simple psychological rejection of the colonizer and his culture was very widespread, but it was not a conscious, rationalized stand; it was an attitude bound up with the cultural tradition of the group, its past struggles with the Portuguese and present experience of subjection.

The Portuguese wish to implant their culture throughout the territory, even if well intentioned, was completely unrealistic because of the numbers involved. Comprising less than 2 per cent of the population, they could not hope to give all the Africans an opportunity of even observing the Portuguese way of life, let alone bring them into close enough contact to absorb it. Like many colonizing nations, they also miscalculated the enthusiasm of the 'poor savages' for 'civilization'. Since most Africans met the Portuguese only when paying taxes, when contracted for forced labour or when having their land seized, it is scarcely surprising that they should have received a very unfavourable impression of Portuguese culture. This revulsion is often expressed in songs, dances, even carvings – traditional forms of expression which the colonizer does not understand, and through which he can thus be secretly ridiculed, denounced and threatened. The Chope, for instance, sing:

We are still angry; it's always the same story
The oldest daughters must pay the tax
Natanele tells the white man to leave him alone
Natanele tells the white man to leave me be
You, the elders must discuss our affairs
For the man the whites appointed is the son of a nobody
The Chope have lost the right to their own land
Let me tell you about it . . .

In another song, they ridicule the attempt to impose Portuguese manners:

Listen to the song of Chigombe village
It's tedious saying *bom dia* all the time
Macarite and Babuane are in prison
Because they didn't say *bom dia*,
They had to go to Quissico to say *bom dia*.

The mercantile values of the European are frequently satirized or attacked:

How it surprised me,
My brother Nguissa,
How it surprised me
To take along money to buy my way.

Some of the carvings of the Makonde people express a deep-seated hostility to the alien culture. In that area, Catholic missionaries have been very active, and under their influence many carvers have made madonnas and crucifixes, imitating European models. Unlike Makonde work on traditional themes, these Christian images are often rigidly stereotyped and lifeless. But sometimes one of them departs from the stereotype, and when it does, this is nearly always because an element of doubt or defiance has been worked into it: a madonna is given a demon to hold instead of the Christ child; a priest is represented with the feet of a wild animal, a pieta becomes a study not of sorrow but of revenge, with the mother raising a spear over the body of her dead son.

In specific areas at specific times, these attitudes, ingrained in popular culture, crystallized into action of one kind or another: the 'elders' did 'discuss our affairs'. One form that this took was the cooperative movement, which developed in the north in the fifties. In its early stages, this was constructive rather than defiant. A number of peasants – including Mzee Lázaro Kavandame, now a member of FRELIMO's Central Committee and Provincial Secretary for Cabo Delgado – organized themselves into cooperatives, in an attempt to rationalize the production and sale of agricultural produce and so improve their economic lot. The Portuguese authorities, however, placed severe restrictions on the activities of the cooperatives, burdened them with financial levies, and kept all their meetings under strict surveillance. It was then that the movement began to acquire a more political character, becoming totally hostile to the authorities.

Early nationalism

Conditions were scarcely favourable for the spread of developed nationalist ideas throughout the country. Because of the ban on political association, the necessity for secrecy which this imposed, the erosion of traditional society and the lack of modern education in rural areas, it was at first only among a tiny minority that the idea of national, as opposed to local, action could gain currency.

This minority was predominantly an urban one, composed of intellectuals and wage-earners, of individuals essentially detribalized, mostly assimilated Africans and mulattos; in other words a tiny marginal section of the population.

In the towns, the colonizing power was seen at close quarters. It was easier there to understand that the colonizer's strength was built upon our weakness, and that their achievements depended on the labour of the African. Possibly the very absence of the tribal environment helped to encourage a national view, helped this group to see Mozambique as the country of all Mozambicans, helped them to understand the power of unity.

Encouraged by the liberalism of the new Republic in Portugal (1910–26), these groups formed societies and started newspapers with which they conducted campaigns against the abuses of colonialism, demanding equal rights, until, little by little, they began to denounce the whole colonial system.

In 1920 the *Liga Africana* was established in Lisbon, as an organization uniting the very few African and mulatto students who came to the city. Its intention was to give 'an organized character to liaisons between colonized peoples'; it participated in the Third Pan African Conference held in London and organized by W. E. Du Bois, and in 1923 received the Second session of the Conference in Lisbon. It was significant that in its conception the *Liga* stood not only for national unity but also for unity between colonies against the same colonial power, a wider African unity against all colonizing powers, and unity among all oppressed black peoples of the world. But in fact it was weak, consisting as it did only of some twenty members and situated in Lisbon, far from the scene of possible action.

In Mozambique in the early twenties, an organization called *Grémio Africano* (African guild) was formed, and this later evolved into the *Associação Africana*. The settlers and the administration soon became alarmed at the strength of the Association's demands, and in the early thirties, favoured by the fascist winds blowing from Portugal, they began a campaign of intimidation and infiltration, and succeeded in gaining the help of some of the leaders to direct the association along more conformist lines. A more radical wing was then formed, which broke away and created the *Instituto Negrófilo*; and this was later forced to change its name by the Salazar government, to *Centro Associativo dos Negros de Moçambique*. A tendency developed for mulattos to join the *Associação Africana*, while black Africans were concentrated in the *Centro Associativo*.

A third organization was formed, called *Associação dos Naturais de Moçambique*. This was originally conceived as a means of defending the rights of whites born in Mozambique; but from the 1950s it opened its doors to other ethnic groups, and after that became quite active in the struggle against racism. It even did a little to advance African education by providing scholarships. Other similar associations were formed by smaller interest groups, like Moslem Africans or different groups of Indians.

All these organizations carried out political action under the cover of social programmes, mutual aid, and cultural or athletic activities. And side by side with these movements there developed a protest press, typified by the paper *O Brado Africano* (the African Cry), which was set up by the *Associação Africana* and directed by the Albasini brothers. This press was muzzled in 1936 by the fascist government's system of press censorship, but until then it formed a fairly effective mouthpiece for revolt.

The spirit of these early movements and the nature of their protest are well illustrated by this *O Brado Africano* editorial of 27 February 1932:

We've had a mouthful of it. We've had to put up with you, to suffer the terrible consequences of your follies, of your demands . . . we can no longer put up with the pernicious effects of your political and administrative decisions. From now on we refuse to make ever greater and ever more useless sacrifices. . . . Enough. . . . We insist that you carry out your fundamental duties not with laws and decrees but with acts. . . . We want to be treated in the same way that you are. We do not aspire to the comforts you surround yourselves with, thanks to our strength. We do not aspire to your refined education . . . even less do we aspire to a life dominated by the idea of robbing your brother. . . . We aspire to our 'savage state' which, however, fills your mouths and your pockets. And we demand something . . . we demand bread and light. . . . We repeat that we do not want hunger or thirst or poverty or a law of discrimination based on colour. . . . We will learn to use the scalpel . . . the gangrene that you spread will infect us and then we will no longer have the strength to take action. Now we have it . . . we, the beasts of burden . . .

From this text clearly emerges a line of demarcation between colonizer and colonized; the latter views himself as a dominated whole and sets himself up against another whole, the colonizing group, with which he contests for power. It is interesting to note the complete rejection of the colonizer's values, the proud assumption of the 'savage state' and the definition of the colonizer's civilization as dominated by 'the robbery of your brother'.

It is true that as yet it is not the demand for national independence which is formulated. This stage of denunciation, though, and the demand for equal rights were necessary in the development of political consciousness towards the demand for independence. It was not until after these preliminary demands had been rejected that a more radical position could be taken.

The establishment of Salazar's New State and the political repression which followed put an end to this wave of political activity. Corruption and internal dissension fomented by the government transformed the organizations into bourgeois clubs, which from then on were frequently required by the authorities to join in the chorus of allegiance to Salazar and his régime.

It was not until the end of the Second World War and the defeat of the major fascist powers, that some renewal of political activity became possible. The changes in power across the world and the resurgency of nationalism, particularly in Africa, had repercussions in the Portuguese territories, despite the continuance of a fascist government in Lisbon and the efforts made by the Portuguese authorities to insulate the areas they controlled against the ideas of self-determination gaining ground elsewhere.

The revolt of the intellectuals

Again it was for the most part only the small educated minority who were in a position to follow world events, who had adequate contacts with the outside world, who had been able to acquire the habit of analytical thought and so the necessary equipment to understand the colonial phenomenon as a whole.

In Mozambique a new generation of insurgents arose, active and determined to struggle on their own terms and not on the terms imposed by the colonial government. They were in a position to see the three essential aspects of their situation: racial discrimination and exploitation within the colonial system; the real weakness of the colonizer; and finally man's social evolution in general, with the contrast between the emergence of black struggle in Africa and America and the mute resistance of their own people.

They could analyse the situation, but it was difficult to do more than this. The field of action was limited first of all by the comprehensive structure of oppression, the insidious police network developed by the fascist state during its long period of strength, and secondly by the lack of contact between the politically conscious urban minority and the mass of the population who bore the brunt of exploitation, who actually suffered forced labour, forced cultivation and the daily threat of violence. It is not surprising therefore that among this minority, resistance first found a purely cultural expression.

The new resistance inspired a movement in all the arts which began during the forties and influenced poets, painters and writers from all the Portuguese colonies. From Mozambique the best-known of these are probably the painters Malangatana and Craveirinha, the short story writer Luis Bernardo Honwana, and the poets José Craveirinha and Noémia de Sousa.

The paintings of Malangatana and José Craveirinha (the nephew of the poet) draw their inspiration from the images of traditional sculpture and from African mythology, binding them into works explosive with themes of liberation and the denunciation of colonial violence.

The short stories of Luis Bernardo Honwana, who has been recognized widely outside Africa as a master of his medium, lead the reader to make the same denunciation through a perceptive detailed analysis of human behaviour. Following a long tradition of artists working under an oppressive government, he sometimes writes in the form of parables, or centres his story around one apparently insignificant concrete event which he uses to illuminate the wider situation.

In the political poetry of the forties and fifties, three themes predominate: the reaffirmation of Africa as the mother country, spiritual home and context of a future nation; the rise of the black man elsewhere in the world, the general call to revolt; and the present sufferings of the ordinary people of Mozambique, under forced labour and in the mines.

The first of these themes is often interwoven with the poet's personal conflicts, the problems arising from his origins and family situation already described in connexion with the social position of the mulatto. In a more generalized form it tries to express the common roots of all Mozambicans in a pre-colonial African past, as in this extract from an early poem by Marcelino dos Santos, 'Here we were born':

The land where we were born
goes back
like time

Our forefathers
were born
and lived
in that land

and they, like the coarse wild grass
were the meagre body's veins
running red, earth's fragrance.

Trees and granite pinnacles

their arms
embraced the earth
in daily work
and sculpting the new world's fertile rocks
began in colour
the great design of life . . .

The best example of the second theme is probably Noémia de Sousa's poem, 'Let my people go', inspired by the struggles of the American Negro:

A warm Mozambican night
and the distant tones of *marimbas* reach me
– firm, constant –
coming, I don't know from where.
In my house of wood and zinc
I turn on the radio and let myself drift, lulled. . . .
But voices from America stir my soul and nerves
And Robeson and Marion sing for me
Negro spirituals from Harlem.
'Let my people go'
– oh let my people go
let my people go –
they say.
I open my eyes and can no longer sleep.
Anderson and Paul sound within me
and they are not the soft voices of a lullaby
Let my people go . . .

The sufferings of the forced labourer and the mine worker
inspired many poems, and there are powerful examples from all
the main poets of the period: de Sousa's 'Magaiça'; Craveirinha's
'Mamparra M'Gaiza', 'Mamana Saquina'; Marcelino dos
Santos's 'A terra Treme'. Those poems, however, are interesting
perhaps less for their power and eloquence than for the terms in
which they state the situation. For they illustrate very vividly the
weakness as well as the strength of the movement to which their
authors belonged. None of these writers had themselves experienced forced labour; none of them was subject to the Native
Labour Code, and they write of it as outsiders, reading their own
intellectualized reactions into the minds of the African miner
and forced labourer. Noémia de Sousa, for instance, writes in
'Magaiça':

Bemused Magaiça lit the lamp
to look for lost illusions
his youth, his health, which stayed behind
deep in the mines of Johannesburg.

Craveirinha, speaking of 'the Chope man' on contract in the
Rand, writes: 'each time he thinks of escape is a week in a gallery
without sun.' But in fact there is no question of 'escape': the

Mozambican contracts for the mines in order to bring back cash for the family and avoid forced labour under even more unfavourable economic terms at home. The very way in which such poems are conceived, in a style of eloquent self-pity, is alien to the African reaction. Compare any of these poems with the Chope songs quoted earlier. It is clear that despite the efforts of their authors to be 'African', the former have taken more from the European tradition than from the African. This indicates the lack of contact existing between these intellectuals and the rest of the country. At that time they were no more in a position to forge a true national movement than were the peasants of Lázaro Kavandame's cooperatives. On the other hand, their strength lay in their enthusiasm and ability, gained partly from their knowledge of European history and revolutionary thinking, to analyse a political situation and express it in clear and vivid terms.

Noémia de Sousa wrote this powerful call to revolt when one of her companions in the movement had been arrested and deported after the strikes of 1947:

But what matter?
They have stolen João from us
but João is us all
Because of that João hasn't left us
João 'was' not, João is and will be
For João is us all, we are a multitude
and the multitude
who can carry off the multitude and lock it in a cage?

In *Black Cry* (*Grito Negro*), Craveirinha achieved perhaps one of the most vivid statements on alienation and revolt ever written. Because of its extremely tight and meaningful musical structure, this poem loses much of its power in translation; but it is worth quoting in full, as it is among the most important and influential works of the time:

I am coal!
You tear me brutally from the ground
and make of me your mine, boss

I am coal
and you burn me, boss
to serve you forever as your driving force
but not forever, boss

I am coal
and must burn
and consume everything in the heat of my combustion

I am coal
and must burn, exploited
burn alive like tar, my brother
until no more your mine, boss

I am coal
and must burn
and consume everything in the fire of my combustion

Yes, boss
I will be your coal!*

Few of Craveirinha's group succeeded in escaping from their isolation and bridging the gap between theory and practice. Noémia de Sousa left Mozambique, has stopped writing poetry, and now lives in Paris; many, including Craveirinha and Honwana, are in prison. Malangatana is still working in Mozambique but closely supervised and harassed by the police. Of all those mentioned here, only Marcelino dos Santos, after a long period of exile in Europe, joined the liberation movement, and since then his poetry has changed and developed under the impetus of the armed struggle. The work of Craveirinha and his companions, however, influenced and inspired a slightly younger generation of intellectuals, many of whom were able to escape the surveillance of the police and have thrown themselves into the liberation movement. There, in the context of the armed struggle, a new literary tradition is taking shape.

This is the generation which grew up after the Second World War and who were at school during the early movement for self-determination elsewhere in Africa. It was at school that they began developing their political ideas and at school that they began to organize themselves. The Portuguese education system

* In Portuguese the words coal, brother, boss, combustion, rhyme: *carvão, irmão, patrão, combustão.*

Dr Eduardo Mondlane, President of FRELIMO, at the Congress in Mozambique, July 1968.

Photo: Basil Davidson

Dr Eduardo Mondlane (left) opening the FRELIMO Congress in the woodlands of northern Mozambique.

Photo: Basil Davidson

At the Congress. Left to right: Alfredo Aywasera, senior commissar of FRELIMO units in Tete Province; Samora Machel, commander of FRELIMO army; Francisco Manganja, military commander in Tete Province; Francisco Chisano, leading member of the FRELIMO executive committee.

Photo: Basil Davidson

The Women's delegation
at the Congress

Two guerrilla officers examining captured Portuguese weapons of West German and Belgian makes.
Photo: Anders Johansson

FRELIMO soldiers
at a guerrilla camp in
Cabo Delgado.
Photo: Anders Johansson

Guerrillas on the move.
Photo: *Anders Johansson*

Dr Eduardo Mondlane
with Uria Simango,
Vice-President of
FRELIMO, at the
Congress.
Photo: Basil Davidson

itself gave them good cause for discontent. Those few Africans and mulattos who reached secondary school only did so with great difficulty. In the predominantly white schools they were constantly subject to discrimination. On top of this, the schools attempted to cut them off from their background, annihilate the values they had been brought up with, and make them 'Portuguese' in consciousness although not in rights. How they failed is illustrated by this account from an African girl who was at a technical school in Lourenço Marques only a few years ago:

Josina Muthemba: The colonialists wanted to deceive us with their teaching; they taught us only the history of Portugal, the geography of Portugal; they wanted to form in us a passive mentality, to make us resigned to their domination. We couldn't react openly, but we were aware of their lie; we knew that what they said was false; that we were Mozambicans and we could never be Portuguese. (F.I.)

In 1949 the secondary school pupils, led by some who had been to South Africa to study, formed the *Núcleo dos Estudantes Africanos Secundários de Moçambique* (NESAM), which was linked to the *Centro Associativo dos Negros de Moçambique*, and which similarly under cover of social and cultural activities, conducted among the youth a political campaign to spread the idea of national independence and encourage resistance to the cultural subjection which the Portuguese imposed. From the first the police kept a close watch on the movement. I myself, as one of the students returned from South Africa who had founded NESAM, was arrested and questioned at some length about our activities in 1949. Nevertheless NESAM managed to survive into the sixties, and even launched a magazine, *Alvor*, which although heavily censored helped to spread the ideas developed at the group's meetings and discussions.

NESAM's effectiveness, like that of all the early organizations, was severely limited by its tiny membership, restricted in this instance to the black African pupils of secondary school level. But in at least three ways it made an important contribution to the revolution. It spread nationalist ideas among the black educated youth. It achieved a certain revaluation of national culture, which counteracted the attempts by the Portuguese to make African students despise and abandon their own people; NESAM provided the only opportunity to study and discuss Mozambique in its own right and not as an appendage of Portugal's. And, most important perhaps, by cementing personal contacts, it established a nation-wide network of communication, which extended among old members as well as those still at school, and which could be used by a future underground. For instance, when FRELIMO established itself in the Lourenço Marques region in 1962–3, the NESAM members were among the first to be mobilized and provided a structure to receive the party. The secret police, PIDE, also understood this and banned NESAM; in 1964 they arrested some of its members and forced others into exile. It was at this time that Josina Muthemba was active in NESAM, and she describes this state of oppression and the fate of her own group:

We wanted to organize ourselves, but we were persecuted by the secret police. We had cultural and educational activities, but during discussions, talks and debates we had to keep a constant lookout for the police. . . . The police persecuted us, they even banned NESAM.

I was also arrested when I was running away from Mozambique. I was arrested at the Victoria Falls on the frontier between Rhodesia and Zambia. The Rhodesian police arrested me and sent me back to Lourenço Marques (the Rhodesian police work closely with the Portuguese police). There were eight of us in our group, boys and girls. The Portuguese police threatened us, interrogated us and beat up the boys. I was in prison for six months without being sentenced or condemned. I was in prison for six months without them bringing a case against me at all. (F.I.)

Shortly after this, seventy-five NESAM members were arrested by the South African police and handed over to PIDE, while they were trying to make their way from Swaziland to Zambia. They are still in concentration camps in southern Mozambique.

In 1963 it was some former NESAM members who created UNEMO, the Mozambican Student Union which is formally a part of FRELIMO, and which organizes Mozambican students studying through FRELIMO auspices.

Within Portugal, the very few black or mulatto students who

reached an institute of higher education gathered in the *Casa dos Estudantes do Imperio* (CEI), and also established a link through the *Club dos Maritimos* with sailors from the colonies who frequently came to Lisbon. In 1951 the *Centro de Estudos Africanos* was formed by CEI members, although not itself a part of CEI. Despite the oppressive measures of the police the CEI worked actively, until its dissolution in 1965, to spread the word of national independence in the colonies, to diffuse information about the colonies to the world beyond Portugal, and to harden and consolidate nationalist ideas among the youth. In 1961 a large group of these students, frustrated and finally threatened by the persistent nature of police action, fled across the border and made their way into France and Switzerland, making a public and irreversible break with the Portuguese régime. Most of these immediately established open contact with their nationalist movements, and a number of these former students of the 'Portuguese Empire' are now among the leaders of FRELIMO.

Industrial action

If it was among the intellectuals that political thought and organization developed furthest during the period following the Second World War, it was among the urban proletariat that the first experiments in organized active resistance took place. The concentration of labour in and near the towns, and the terrible working conditions and poverty, provided the fundamental impetus to revolt; but in the absence of trade unions, it was only clandestine political groups which could provide the organization necessary. The only unions permitted by the Portuguese are the fascist unions, whose leaders are chosen by the employers and the state, and who, in any event, extend membership only to whites and occasionally to assimilated Africans.

In 1947 the radical discontent of the labour force, combined with political agitation, produced a series of strikes, in the docks of Lourenço Marques and in neighbouring plantations, which culminated in an abortive uprising at Lourenço Marques in 1948. The participants were punished ferociously, and several hundred Africans were deported to São Tomé. In 1956, again at

Lourenço Marques, there was a dock strike which ended in the death of forty-nine participants. Then, in 1962–3, the FRELIMO underground took over the work of organization and set up a more coordinated system, which helped to plan the series of dock strikes which broke out in 1963 at Lourenço Marques, Beira and Nacala. Despite its wider extent, this last effort also ended only in the death and arrest of many participants. Although some political organization existed among the workers responsible for the strikes, the strike action itself was very largely spontaneous and for the most part localized. Its failure and the brutal repression which followed in every instance have temporarily discouraged both the masses and the leadership from considering strike action as a possible effective political weapon in the context of Mozambique.

Towards unity

Both the agitation of the intellectuals and the strikes of the urban labour force were doomed to failure, because in both cases it was the action only of a tiny isolated group. For a government like Portugal's, which has set its face against democracy and is prepared to use extremes of brutality to crush opposition, it is easy to deal with such isolated pockets of resistance. It was the very failure of these attempts, however, and the fierce repression which followed, that made this clear and prepared the ground for more widely based action. The urban population of Mozambique amounts altogether to less than half a million. A nationalist movement without firm roots in the countryside could never hope to succeed.

Some developments in the countryside which took place in the period just preceding the formation of FRELIMO were of enormous importance. These took the most extreme direction in the northern area around Mueda, though they had their milder counterparts in other regions. They were first of all the effect on the population of the failure of the cooperative movement already described. The reaction of the leaders is best illustrated in the words of Lázaro Kavandame himself:

I couldn't sleep all night. I knew that from that moment they wouldn't leave me in peace, that everything I did would be closely watched and controlled by the authorities; that they would call me more and more often to the administrative post and that I would be constantly watched by the police. My only hope was to run away. . . . We immediately made arrangements to organize a meeting of the people's leaders to discuss what we should do to regain our liberty and to drive the Portuguese oppressors out of our country. After a long and important discussion, we reached the conclusion that the Makonde people alone could not succeed in driving out the enemy. We then decided to join forces with Mozambicans from the rest of the country. [Official report.]

The other development, also associated with the cooperatives, was an increase in spontaneous agitation, which culminated in a major demonstration at Mueda in 1960. This demonstration, though passing unnoticed by the rest of the world, acted as a catalyst on the region. Over 500 people were shot down by the Portuguese, and many who up to that time had not considered the use of violence now denounced peaceful resistance as futile. The experience of Teresinha Mblale, now a FRELIMO militant, shows why: 'I saw how the colonialists massacred the people at Mueda. That was when I lost my uncle. Our people were unarmed when they began to shoot.' She was one of the thousands who determined never again to be unarmed in the face of Portuguese violence.

A fuller account of that day comes from Alberto-Joaquim Chipande, then aged 22, and now one of the leaders in Cabo Delgado:

Certain leaders worked amongst us. Some of them were taken by the Portuguese – Tiago Muller, Faustino Vanomba, Kibiriti Diwane – in the massacre at Mueda on 16 June 1960. How did that happen ? Well, some of these men had made contact with the authorities and asked for more liberty and more pay. . . . After a while, when people were giving support to these leaders, the Portuguese sent police through the villages inviting people to a meeting at Mueda. Several thousand people came to hear what the Portuguese would say. As it turned out, the administrator had asked the governor of Delgado Province to come from Porto Amélia and to bring a company of troops. But these

117

troops were hidden when they got to Mueda. We didn't see them at first.

Then the governor invited our leaders into the administrator's office. I was waiting outside. They were in there for four hours. When they came out on the verandah, the governor asked the crowd who wanted to speak. Many wanted to speak, and the governor told them all to stand on one side.

Then without another word he ordered the police to bind the hands of those who had stood on one side, and the police began beating them. I was close by. I saw it all. When the people saw what was happening, they began to demonstrate against the Portuguese, and the Portuguese simply ordered the police trucks to come and collect these arrested persons. So there were more demonstrations against this. At that moment the troops were still hidden, and the people went up close to the police to stop the arrested persons from being taken away. So the governor called the troops, and when they appeared he told them to open fire. They killed about 600 people. Now the Portuguese say they have punished that governor, but of course they have only sent him somewhere else. I myself escaped because I was close to a graveyard where I could take cover, and then I ran away. (D.I.)

After this massacre things in the north could never return to normal. Throughout the region it had aroused the most bitter hatred against the Portuguese and showed once and for all that peaceful resistance was futile.

Thus everywhere it was the very severity of repression that created the necessary conditions for the development of a strong, militant nationalist movement. The tight police state drove all political action underground, and – partly because of the difficulties and dangers involved – underground activity turned out to be the best school in which to form a body of tough, devoted and radical political workers. The excesses of the régime destroyed all possibility of reforms which, by improving conditions a little, might have secured the main interests of colonial rule from a serious attack for some time to come.

The first attempts to create a nation-wide radical nationalist movement were made by Mozambicans working in neighbouring countries, where they were beyond the immediate reach of PIDE. At first the old problem of inadequate communications led to the establishment of three separate movements:

UDENAMO (*União Nacional Democrática de Moçambique*) formed in 1960 in Salisbury; MANU (*Mozambique African National Union*) formed in 1961 from a number of smaller groups already existing among Mozambicans working in Tanganyika and Kenya, one of the largest being the Mozambique Makonde Union; UNAMI (*União Africana de Moçambique Independente*) started by exiles from the Tete region living in Malawi.

The accession of many former colonies to independence in the late fifties and early sixties favoured the formation of 'exile' movements, and for Mozambique, Tanganyika's independence, gained in 1961, seemed to offer new scope. All three movements established separate headquarters in Dar es Salaam soon afterwards.

In 1961, too, an intensification of repression in all the Portuguese territories followed the revolt in Angola and caused an influx of refugees into neighbouring countries, particularly Tanganyika (now Tanzania). These recent exiles from the interior, many of whom did not already belong to any of the existing organizations, exercised strong pressure for the formation of a single united body. External conditions also favoured unity: the Conference of the Nationalist Organizations of the Portuguese Territories (CONCP) held at Casablanca in 1961 and attended by UDENAMO made a strong call for the unity of nationalist movements against Portuguese colonialism. A conference of all nationalist movements, called by Ghana's President Kwame Nkrumah, also encouraged the formation of united fronts, and in Tanganyika President Nyerere personally exerted influence on the movements established in the territory to unite. Thus on 25 June 1962 the three movements in Dar es Salaam merged to form the Mozambique Liberation Front (FRELIMO), and preparations were made to hold a conference in the following September which would define the aims of the Front and work out a programme for action.

A brief account of a few among the leaders of the new movement will illustrate how various political and para-political organizations from all over the country contributed to it. The Vice-President, the Reverend Uria Simango, is a Protestant pastor from the Beira region who had been involved in the mutual aid associations and was the leader of UDENAMO. Also from the mutual aid association of the Beira region came Silverio Nungu, later FRELIMO Secretary for Administration, and Samuel Dhlakama, now a member of the Central Committee. From the peasant cooperatives of northern Mozambique came Lázaro Kavandame, later Provincial Secretary for Cabo Delgado; also Jonas Namashulua, and others. From the mutual assistance associations of Lourenço Marques and Chai Chai in the south of Mozambique came the late Mateus Muthemba, and Shaffrudin M. Khan, who became FRELIMO representative in Cairo and is now representative in the United States. Marcelino dos Santos, later FRELIMO Secretary for External Affairs and now Secretary of the Department of Political Affairs, is a poet of international standing; he was active in the literary movement in Lourenço Marques and then spent some years of exile in France.

I myself am from the Gaza district of southern Mozambique, and, like many of us, my involvement with resistance of one form or another goes back to my childhood. I began life, as most Mozambican children do, in a village, and until the age of ten I spent my days herding the family livestock with my brothers and absorbing the traditions of my tribe and family. That I went to school at all I owe to the far-sightedness of my mother, who was my father's third and last wife, and a woman of considerable character and intelligence. In trying to continue my education after primary school, I experienced all the frustrations and difficulties in store for an African child attempting to enter the Portuguese system. Eventually I managed to reach South Africa, and with the help of some of my teachers I continued studying on scholarships to college level. It was during this period that my work with NESAM, and so my serious troubles with the police, began. When I was offered a scholarship to America, the Portuguese authorities decided to send me to Lisbon University instead. During my brief stay there, however, I was harassed so constantly by the police that it interfered with my studies, and I made efforts to take up my scholarship in the United States. Succeeding, I studied sociology and anthropology at Oberlin and

Northwestern Universities, and then worked for the United Nations as a research officer in the Trusteeship section.

Meanwhile I kept in touch as far as possible with developments in Mozambique, and I became increasingly convinced from what I saw and from my occasional contacts through the UN with the Portuguese diplomats that normal political pressure and agitation would not affect the Portuguese stand. In 1961 I was able to visit Mozambique on leave from the UN, and travelling widely saw for myself how conditions had changed, or not changed, since I had left. On my return I left the United Nations to engage openly in the liberation struggle, and took a job lecturing at Syracuse University which left me the time and the opportunity to study the situation further. I had established contacts with all the separate liberation parties, but I had refused to join any of them separately, and was among those campaigning strongly for unity in 1961 and 1962.

The Mozambicans who gathered in Dar es Salaam in 1962 together represented almost every region of Mozambique and every sector of the population. Nearly everyone had some experience of resistance on a small scale, and of the reprisals which normally followed. Both inside and outside the country, conditions were favourable to the nationalist struggle. Our problem was whether we could weld together these advantages so as to make our movement strong throughout the country, and capable of taking effective action which, unlike previous isolated efforts, would hurt the Portuguese more than it hurt us.

6 Consolidation

It is clear that we Portuguese are forewarned and it will not be possible for agents ... to repeat in Mozambique the vile exploits of agents in Angola. He who is forewarned doubles his defences.
Diário da Manhã, 12 September 1964

After September 1962 we had a single party and the bones of a policy, but we were still a long way from having an effective national liberation struggle. It took two years of hard work, planning and learning from our mistakes and failures before we were able to set out confidently on an active path towards liberation.

At the First Congress of FRELIMO, the aims of the party were defined:

The Congress of FRELIMO –
Having examined the present needs of the struggle against Portuguese colonialism in Mozambique – declares its firm determination to promote the efficient organization of the struggle of the Mozambican people for national liberation, and adopts the following resolutions to be put into immediate execution by the Central Committee of FRELIMO:

1. To develop and consolidate the organizational structure of FRELIMO;

2. to further the unity of Mozambicans;

3. to achieve maximum utilization of the energies and capacities of each and every member of FRELIMO;

4. to promote and accelerate training of cadres;

5. to employ directly every effort to promote the rapid access of Mozambique to independence;

6. to promote by every method the social and cultural development of the Mozambican woman;

7. to promote at once the literacy of the Mozambican people, creating schools wherever possible;

8. to take the necessary measures towards supplying the needs of the organs of different levels of FRELIMO;

9. to encourage and support the formation and consolidation of trade union, student, youth and women's organizations;

10. to cooperate with the nationalist organizations of the other Portuguese colonies;

11. to cooperate with African nationalist organizations;

12. to cooperate with the nationalist movements of all countries;

13. to obtain funds from organizations which sympathize with the cause of the people of Mozambique, making public appeals;

14. to procure all requirements for self defence and resistance of the Mozambican people;

15. to organize permanent propaganda by all methods in order to mobilize world public opinion in favour of the cause of the Mozambican people;

16. to send delegations to all countries in order to undertake campaigns and public demonstrations of protest against the atrocities committed by the Portuguese colonial administration, as well as to press for the immediate liberation of all nationalists who are inside the Portuguese colonialist prisons;

17. to procure diplomatic, moral and material help for the cause of the Mozambican people from the African states and from all peace and freedom loving people.

These aims could be summarized as consolidation and mobilization; preparation for war; education; diplomacy.

The need for an armed struggle

Although determined to do everything in our power to try to gain independence by peaceful means, we were already convinced at this stage that a war would be necessary. People more familiar with the policies of other colonial powers have accused us of resorting to violence without due cause. This is partly refuted by the fate met by every type of legal, democratic and reformist activity tried over the preceding forty years.

The character of the government in Portugal itself makes a peaceful solution inherently unlikely. Within Portugal the government has promoted neither sound economic growth nor social well-being, and has gained little international respect. The possession of colonies has helped to conceal these failures: the colonies contribute to the economy; they add to Portugal's consequence in the world, particularly the world of finance; they have provided a national myth of empire which helps discourage any grumbling by a fundamentally dissatisfied population. The government knows how ill it can afford to lose the colonies. For similar reasons it cannot afford to liberalize its control of them: the colonies contribute to the metropolitan economy only because labour is exploited and resources are not ploughed back into local development; the colonies ease the discontent of the Portuguese population only because immigration offers to the poor and uneducated a position of special privilege. Not least, since the fascist government has eliminated democracy within Portugal itself, it can scarcely allow a greater measure of freedom to the supposedly more backward people of its colonies.

Despite all this, attempts were made to use persuasion, encouraged by the acceptance elsewhere of the principle of self-determination. But such efforts were never rewarded with any kind of 'dialogue'. The only reaction to them was prison, censorship, and the strengthening of the PIDE, the secret police. The character of the PIDE is itself an important factor. For it has a strong tradition of violence – its officers were trained by the Gestapo – and it enjoys a considerable measure of autonomy, allowing it to act outside the control of the official law.

This is why political activity in Mozambique has called for the techniques of the 'underground', for secrecy and exile. On the only recent occasion when an open approach was made, what happened is instructive. It was the incident, already mentioned, at Mueda in 1960, when some 500 Africans were killed. It had been planned as a peaceful demonstration and to some extent owed its origin to police provocation: the authorities knew that there was political agitation in the region, much of it clandestine, and they had given out that the governor would attend a public meeting on 16 June where he would grant independence to the Makonde people. The police thus brought the disaffection into the open and immediately killed or arrested as many as they could of those involved. They had hoped to remove the leaders, intimidate the population and set an example to other regions. But despite its ferocity, the action was only partially and temporarily successful. It eliminated some of the leaders, but others remained; while, far from being intimidated, the population became more determined than ever to resist.

Some of the exiles and those involved in clandestine opposition hoped at first that, even if Portugal was impervious to peaceful demands from the people of her colonies, she might listen to international organizations and the great nations of the world, if these would intervene on our behalf. Stemming from the Goan issue, some international pressure was brought to bear on Portugal during the fifties. But Portugal's only response was the legislation of the early sixties, which supposedly introduced reforms but made no concession to the principle of self-determination. Since then Portugal has ignored or rejected all appeals from other states or international bodies made on behalf of the people in her colonies. Besides this, not all the major states support us. Since 1961 most Western powers, including the United States, have not cooperated with United Nations resolutions urging Portugal to give the right of self-determination to the people of her non-self-governing territories.

By 1961 two conclusions were obvious. First, Portugal would not admit the principle of self-determination and independence, or allow for any extension of democracy under her own rule, although by then it was clear that her own 'Portuguese' solutions to our oppressed condition, such as assimilation by multi-racial *colonatos*, multi-racial schools, local elections etc., had proved a meaningless fraud. Secondly, moderate political action such as strikes, demonstrations and petitions, would result only in the destruction of those who took part in them. We were, therefore, left with these alternatives: to continue indefinitely living under a repressive imperial rule, or to find a means of using force against Portugal which would be effective enough to hurt Portugal without resulting in our own ruin.

This was why, to FRELIMO leaders, armed action appeared to be the only method. Indeed, the absence of any opposition to the use of force was one of the factors accounting for the very short period which elapsed between the formation of FRELIMO in 1962 and the beginning of the armed struggle on 25 September 1964.

Preparation

To create conditions for a successful armed struggle we had, on the one hand, to prepare the population inside Mozambique; and, on the other, to recruit and train people for the responsibilities which such a struggle would impose.

There already existed within Mozambique the makings of a structure through which the work of preparation could proceed. Almost all those who gathered in Dar es Salaam to form FRELIMO were part of underground forces inside Mozambique; the three parties which merged had members in various regions, and these, together with the NESAM network and the people who had taken part in the abortive cooperative movement in Northern Mozambique, formed the basis of an organization which then had to be consolidated and expanded. Through this, the aims of the party had to be explained to the population; the people had to be organized into cells, the general level of political consciousness raised, the activity of the cells coordinated. This was done by underground workers using pamphlets and 'bush telegrams' as aids.

The way that such a mobilization campaign works is perhaps best illustrated by some accounts from present FRELIMO militants of how they came to join the party. As Joaquim Maquival puts it:

In 1964 I joined FRELIMO because our people were exploited. I still did not know properly what to do about it. The people didn't know what to do. We had heard our neighbours in Malawi had been liberated and would come to liberate us, but we soon learnt that we would have to liberate ourselves. The party told us that we and no one else are responsible for ourselves.

Some comrades came to explain things to us, and before, right at the beginning, the radio told us that FRELIMO, led by Comrade Mondlane, was fighting for the liberation of us all. (F.I.)

Gabriel Maurício Nantimbo has a similar story:

> Previously I was in a state of servitude, but I didn't know it. I thought that was just how the world was. I didn't know that Mozambique was our country. The books said we were Portuguese. Then about 1961 I began to hear other things. The old men in their cooperatives were also beginning to agitate. In 1962 even the children saw the truth. FRELIMO began operating in our zone. Some comrades explained about it and I wanted to join. By the end of 1962 even the government felt that the party was growing, and they started a great campaign of repression, arresting and torturing everyone they suspected. Many preferred to die rather than betray their comrades. The party gained strength. The leaders explained the truth to us, taught us our own strength, and we saw clearly how Mozambique, which belongs to us and not to Portugal, had been dominated. (F.I.)

Favourable conditions already existed: the suffering caused by the colonial system; the desire to take action; the courage and determination that a war demands. All FRELIMO had to provide was the practical understanding and the organization.

Similar work could be done more openly among the large numbers who fled from Mozambique at about this time. Many of these refugees were eager to return and take action against the system that had driven them out; they lacked only the knowledge of how to do it.

The problem of training involved not only the military aspect. The deficiencies of the Portuguese educational system meant that our movement was desperately short of trained cadres in all fields. We could see that the success of future armed action would create the need for people with a variety of technical skills and a certain level of basic education. Moreover, the state of ignorance in which almost the whole population had been kept hindered the development of a political consciousness and would clearly hinder yet further the development of our country after independence. We had, and have, the task of making up for years of diligent neglect under the Portuguese. And so a military programme and an educational programme were conceived side by side as essential aspects of our struggle.

As a first step in the educational programme, a secondary school, the Mozambique Institute, was established in 1963 at

Dar es Salaam to provide education for Mozambican children who had already left Mozambique, while at the same time scholarships to foreign institutes of higher studies were arranged for those refugees who possessed suitable qualifications.

The persecution and suppression of NESAM had driven out many of those few Africans who had been able to pursue their studies beyond primary school inside Mozambique. Some of these were eager to join the struggle immediately, using such qualifications as they already had; but others were sent to continue their studies and gain qualifications which would be useful in the future. The Mozambique Institute expanded rapidly. Built to take only fifty students, it had been stretched to accommodate 120 by 1968. In addition, the educational department of FRELIMO was able to use the organization of the Institute to help prepare an educational system for use inside Mozambique as soon as the military programme had developed far enough to provide the necessary security.

On the military side, the first task was to train the core of our future army. We approached Algeria, which had just gained independence from France at the end of a seven-year war and was already training nationalist groups from other Portuguese colonies. The Algerian leaders agreed to include Mozambicans in this programme, and the first group of about fifty young Mozambicans went to Algeria in January 1963, followed shortly by two other groups of about seventy. To follow up this training, coordinate the groups and prepare them to fight inside Mozambique, it was necessary to find a country close by the area of prospective fighting which would permit us to establish at least one camp on its territory. It should be stressed that this is a very serious matter. Any country, which agrees to become host to such a military force, even temporarily, must face considerable problems. First is the internal problem posed by the presence of an armed force which is not directly under the country's control. Then there are the diplomatic and security difficulties to be faced as soon as the government against which the military preparations are directed discovers the existence of such a camp. Thus, when Tanganyika agreed to help us, it was taking a very courageous step.

There is a certain historical irony in the siting of our first camp near the village of Bagamoyo. For the name 'Bagamoyo' means 'broken heart' and originates from the time of the slave trade, when this village was one of the main points of departure for the slaving ports of the East Coast. Later, the same town became the capital of the German imperialist venture in East Africa. The name now has acquired for us a completely different significance, for it was here in Bagamoyo that we were able to take the first practical steps towards stamping out servitude in our country.

Once the first groups had undergone further stringent training in Bagamoyo, they returned in secret to Mozambique, prepared for action, and for training other young people. By May 1964 arms were being introduced to Mozambique, and ammunition stocked.

The army also has a major part to play in the mobilization and educational campaigns. Militants learn more than just military science. As far as possible they are taught Portuguese and basic literacy, with those who have already had a little education frequently teaching their comrades. Political education is a very important part of their training, and in the course of it they acquire some experience of speaking in public and of working on committees, while also learning the rudiments of political argument and the historical and geographical background of the struggle. Thus the army itself becomes an important agent in the political mobilization and education of the population.

The other main aspect of FRELIMO's work during this period of preface was a programme of diplomacy and information. The aim of this was, on the one hand, to break through the silence which enveloped Mozambique, to debunk the myths spread by the powerful propaganda services of the Portuguese; and, on the other hand, to mobilize world opinion in favour of the struggle in Mozambique, to gain material support and to isolate Portugal. This involved active participation in international organizations, the dispatch of delegates to international conferences and representatives to various countries. To facilitate this work, permanent offices were set up outside Tanzania, particularly in Cairo, Algiers and Lusaka. To propagate information, papers were prepared for conferences and meetings; articles were written; and from the office in Dar es Salaam the publication began of a regular bulletin in English, *Mozambique Revolution*, while a bulletin in French appeared periodically from the Algiers office.

Problems

In many ways the period of preparation puts more strains on a movement than does the time of action. Once fighting begins, solidarity is generated in the face of immediate danger from the enemy. Also, the movement is able to prove itself: it can show concrete results for its work and a practical justification of its policy. As it proves itself, the enthusiasm and confidence of its own members grows, while at the same time outside interest and support increase. During the time of secret underground work, however, there is little to be seen of the party except a name, an office and a group of exiles who claim to be national leaders but whose integrity is always open to question. It is then that a movement is especially vulnerable to internal dissension and outside provocation.

For FRELIMO in its first two years, the potential danger was aggravated by the inexperience of its leaders in working together. Many of its members also lacked an understanding of modern politics. On the other hand, the problem of maintaining unity was eased by the fact that there were no other parties in existence. After the union of 1962, our problem was not one of bringing together major rival groups but of preventing factions from developing within.

The heterogeneous nature of the membership carried certain dangers as well as advantages. We came from all over Mozambique and from all walks of life: different language and ethnic groups were represented, different races, different religions, different social and political backgrounds. The occasions for possible conflict were unlimited, and we found that we had to make a conscious effort to preserve unity. The main form this took was education. From the very beginning we carried on political education to combat tribalism, racism and religious intolerance. Portuguese was retained as the official language mainly for convenience, as no African language has the wide currency in Mozambique that Swahili, for instance, has in Tanzania. Work, however, is also often carried on in other languages, and the fact that people from different areas are constantly working together has encouraged the learning of these. From the outset, military units were always very mixed in composition, and the experience of working together with people from other tribes did a great deal to lessen tribal friction. FRELIMO is an entirely secular body; within it all religions are tolerated, and a great variety practised.

There was, all the same, shortly after the formation of FRELIMO, a tendency for individuals to claim to represent Mozambique and form bogus, splinter organizations. This seemed mainly due to the conjunction of certain personal ambitions with the manoeuvres of the Portuguese and other interests threatened by the liberation movement. Early on, COSERU (*Comité Secreto de Restanração da* UDENAMO) appeared, and then gave place to a New UDENAMO, which then split into New UDENAMO–Accra, and New UDENAMO–Cairo; both of these have since disappeared. In addition, there emerged a new UNAMI (now vanished), a new MANU, and yet more variations on the theme. The individuals forming these different organizations were often the same. Then, in 1964, a group called MORECO (Mozambican Revolutionary Council) was formed, which later changed into COREMO and almost immediately underwent further upheaval, as the Chairman and the National President, the General Secretary and the Plenipotentiary Secretary, each expelled the other. There is now a branch of COREMO in Lusaka and a branch in Cairo which seem to be separated by ideological differences. COREMO–Lusaka has recently undergone another split, which resulted in the formation of yet another group called *União Nacional Africana da Rombézia*. UNAR's programme aims at weakening the work of FRELIMO in the area between the two main rivers of north Mozambique, the Zambezi and the Rovuma. At the most charitable estimate, the leaders of the group must be naïve to take seriously the rumours, fanned by the Portuguese, that they would be ready to hand over the northern third of the country to Malawi if, by that manoeuvre, they would be assured of perpetual control over the two-thirds of Mozambique from the Zambezi southwards. It is significant that the headquarters of UNAR is in Blantyre, and that the leaders enjoy the protection and cooperation of some influential figures in the Malawi Congress Party.

COREMO–Lusaka is the only one of these groups which has attempted any action inside Mozambique: in 1965, COREMO supporters started military action in Tete, but they were crushed immediately. It seemed that no groundwork had been done on which to base such action; as a result of the repression which followed, some 6,000 people fled to Zambia, and the government of Zambia at first assumed that, as the action had been instigated by COREMO, these were COREMO supporters. After questioning them, however, they found that they had not heard of COREMO, and that those who were attached to any party were members of FRELIMO.

None of these splinter movements was, fortunately, serious enough to interfere with work inside Mozambique, as most of them consisted of just an office and a small group of exile supporters. At that time, however, when all FRELIMO had to show outsiders was a number of officers, there was a risk that they might do some damage beyond. The proliferation of small opposition groups was an embarrassment to the countries which offered support to liberation movements, since it was not easy to tell at first which groups had real backing within Mozambique.

Another difficulty, particularly acute in the early stages of development, when many of the movement's members know little about one another, is the danger of infiltration by Portuguese agents. And this is connected with the problem of splinter groups, since these may use a member of the main organization to try to spread dissent, so as to bring over a section of the membership. The complexity of motives behind divisive conduct makes it the more difficult to guard against: individual neuroses, personal ambitions, real ideological differences are muddled up with the tactics of the enemy secret service. A movement cannot afford to become too paranoiac, or it will alienate potential support and fail to reconcile those real differences that somehow must be reconciled if its broad basis is to survive and develop. On the other hand, it must guard against the more dangerous type of infiltration organized by its enemies, inevitably expending time and energy in the process.

The best answer to splinter groups, agents, spies, inflammatory propagandists, is a strong movement. If the leadership is united and is based on mass support in the country; if the programme is realistic and popular, then the damage which such outside efforts can achieve will be marginal. In F R E L I M O, although in some instances specific action may have to be taken, our general policy is simply to press on with the main work in hand, ignoring petty provocations.

A political biography

So long as the leadership outside the country could preserve a reasonable degree of unity, the main work inside Mozambique could continue unchecked. The way in which it did so during these years, culminating in the launching of the armed struggle, and some of the problems in the development of the movement, can be seen in greater detail through the personal story of Alberto-Joaquim Chipande:

My father was a *capitão mor* (a village lineage head in a society without centralized political institutions). But sometimes the Portuguese used to give their orders through him, although he wasn't a *regulo* (a chief imposed by the Portuguese). Twice my father was taken to see Lisbon, once in 1940 and again in 1946, and you could say that in a way he was even a member of the Portuguese administration; but he was secretly against them and in 1962 he became a secret member of F R E L I M O when we were still working underground in Delgado . . .

I myself decided to join the struggle because every man should be free, or if he has to, should fight to be free. Ever since I was a child I saw the meaning of Portuguese rule: even when I was twelve (in 1950) and at primary school, they took me and forced me to work in Mueda, cleaning the town.

Then the Portuguese began to track down my family. Two brothers

got away to Tanzania. They escaped after arrest for forced labour. . . .
That was in 1947. I was nine. Then my sister and her husband also
ran away from forced labour. All this taught me. But I stayed at
school. I passed examinations. I became a teacher.

When I finished primary school I was sixteen. Then later I was given
a teaching post. . . . Then I got a better post in Mueda in the primary
school and I stayed there for six years.

I first heard about a certain organization for liberation in 1960.
That was MANU. . . . Certain leaders worked amongst us. Some of
them were taken by the Portuguese at the massacre at Mueda on
16 June 1960. . . . After that experience I had a still stronger feeling
for the need to get our liberty. And when everyone else considered
what had happened they began to act as well, and they supported
MANU.

Then in 1962, when FRELIMO was formed in Dar es Salaam,
its leaders invited some delegates from inside Delgado to go and talk
with them. People who had previously supported MANU began
supporting FRELIMO just as they do today.

After the formation of FRELIMO I became an organizer inside
Delgado. This is how we worked. We had formed an agricultural
cooperative at Mueda, and when FRELIMO's leaders knew of this
they sent delegates inside Delgado to ask the leaders of our cooperative who had been supporters of MANU to support FRELIMO.
They told the delegates of FRELIMO about the reasons for the
formation of MANU and agreed that they would use the cooperative
as long as possible as a means of political organization. We had only a
few people in the first year, and then in the second year we cultivated
cotton. We called our cooperative the Mozambique African Voluntary
Cotton Society. But the Portuguese authorities said we couldn't use
the word *voluntário*, because the blacks, they said, couldn't do anything.
Still they let us try to work and we began. That was in 1957. . . . And
our cooperative developed. Many joined; and so the Portuguese
company (in Mueda) got short of labour, and we began selling our
cotton even to that company. We leaders worked hard and voluntarily;
we took no percentage of the crop, we had no profit in money. All we
leaders had our own *shambas* for our own support. Then that Portuguese company complained to the authorities that our cooperative was
really an anti-Portuguese political organization. In 1959 the leader
– Lázaro Kavandame – was arrested and sent to Porto Amélia. But we
weren't demoralized; we continued. Then the massacre occurred and
they banned our cooperative movement.

At the end of 1960, Lázaro came back, and we talked things over about how to find new ways of working. The authorities said they would allow no organization with many members in it – 30 was the most they would allow. We agreed to that and founded a cooperative with 25 members to grow rice. In the first year we produced a good harvest, we had money in the savings bank, enough to pay wages and we also bought a tractor. ... In 1962, after the formation of FRELIMO, people began giving active support. We had many contacts with Dar through secret messengers, and we began issuing membership cards. We started organizing people. Some of them were arrested, and again we came under government suspicion.

This time it was different. Now the Portuguese wanted our groups to work for the destruction of FRELIMO. They said that we should send men to Dar to create confusion. We sent our vice-chairman, and the Portuguese gave him money for his journey. But we gave him a different task. We gave him a letter to the leaders in Dar to explain why he had the money, and this money we told him to give to FRELIMO and we found the necessary money ourselves. So really this man went to Dar as a delegate to the First Congress of FRELIMO while pretending to the Portuguese to be their agent. He came back after the Congress and told the Portuguese that there were conflicts in Dar between the various groupings in FRELIMO ...

Then he went again in September as our delegate. But this time it went wrong. The Portuguese weren't so simple as to accept what he said just like that. They sent our comrade again, but they also sent another man to spy on him. ... When our comrade came back, he went again to the Portuguese and told them nothing had changed – the groups in Dar still couldn't agree with each other; but the real spy had meanwhile given the Portuguese a very different and real report. So after our comrade came back the second time, the Portuguese started arresting and interrogating our comrades – that was in January 1963. In February they arrested Lázaro, the chairman of FRELIMO in our region, and the next day they arrested our comrade who'd been the delegate.

...

After that there were many arrests, and PIDE agents were all over the place. Many died in prison; others came back with broken health. We had a comrade working in the administrator's office at Mueda. He warned us by letter about those who were going to be arrested. ... On 13 February, early in the morning, the administrator of Mueda came with armed police to the Catholic mission where I was a teacher. ... But we – Lourenço Raimundo, also a secretary of our cooperative, and I – had decided not to sleep there. We made off when we heard the noise of the trucks coming. We stayed all day in the bush, and when night fell we walked to Tanzania. We walked from the thirteenth till the eighteenth, and then that night we crossed the Rovuma into Tanzania.

We got to Lindi and there we were met by a representative of FRELIMO. We told him what had happened. Many refugees came too at that time, because of the Portuguese repression. We held a meeting and decided that some members of our cooperative should go back into Mozambique, because we knew it was our duty to mobilize people, and that without us the people would not have leaders. We decided that the partly educated younger men should go to Dar for further training, while the older men should go back into Mozambique and hide there to go on with mobilization . . .

In Dar the leaders asked us what we wanted to do. We said, to join the army. They asked us, didn't we want scholarships ? No, we said, to fight. So our leaders made contacts with countries ready to help, and the first was Algeria. In June 1963 we went to Algeria and trained there until the spring of 1964. On 4 June we got orders, 24 of us, to meet the President of FRELIMO, and he told us we were chosen for a mission. Next day we went down to Mtwara. On 15 August we were ordered by the representative of FRELIMO to leave that night. We crossed the frontier, and there inside Delgado we found waiting for us the arms and equipment for my group, six French machine-guns, five Thompsons, seven British rifles, six French rifles, twelve pistols, five cases of hand grenades each with twelve. . . . We took these and started for the South, through the forest, but with orders not to begin till we had the word from our leaders. . . . We were not to attack Portuguese civilians, not to maltreat prisoners, not to steal, to pay for what we ate . . .

There were three groups altogether. My group had orders to go towards Porto Amélia. The second, under António Saido, went towards Montepuez, and the third group, Raimundo's, went towards Mueda.

We found it hard, because the enemy was patrolling day and night along the roads and even the bush paths. At one point my group had to wait a couple of days before we could get past. We had good contacts, but because of the Portuguese patrols, it was arranged that at dangerous points only one man should receive us. We suffered from food shortage. And we had to take off our boots for fear of leaving tracks for the Portuguese to follow; we walked barefoot.

It was difficult. At one point there had been at work a bunch of bandits – men who'd been in MANU or UDENAMO and refused to join FRELIMO; they'd simply degenerated into bandits. They'd killed a Dutch missionary. We'd got to a place about five kilometres away. The Portuguese troops backed by aeroplanes were busy there because of the missionary. We took a risk. We made contact with the Dutch missionary's parent mission, and we explained to them what had happened and that FRELIMO was an honest organization and against anything like killing missionaries. This helped, because the missionaries then persuaded the Portuguese that it was so and that they shouldn't kill people in revenge.

We advanced to Macomia. From there we couldn't get on to Porto Amélia, because the Portuguese had set up a blockade and they'd mobilized the people against the bandits. ... The bandits used to pillage Indian shops, and the Portuguese said that we were like that. This held us back. The Indians informed the Portuguese of our tracks. We came to the conclusion that we should start the struggle. We were already fifteen days' walk from the frontier with Tanzania. So while there in Macomia, not able to get any further and wanting to start, we sent messengers to the other two groups for information, and also to Dar, to tell them the details of the situation and explain the dangers of delaying while the armed bandits were around. From these messengers we learnt that the second group had also met with difficulties and hadn't got through to Montpuez; but Raimundo and his group did get through to the outskirts of Mueda.

On 16 September we got our orders from Dar to begin on 25 September; that was at a meeting of our group leaders. We decided that each should go to his own area and begin. Through organizers we planned that the people should rise at the same time – a real national insurrection. To defend the people after that, each group should form militias and explain things to the villagers, while also sabotaging the roads, and, of course, attacking the Portuguese soldiers and administration. That was the outline of the plan we made ...

7 The War

Today's mission
comrade

is, dig the basic soil of Revolution
and make a strong people grow
with a P.M., a bazooka, a 12.7 . . .
From the poem ' To point a moral to a comrade' by Marcelino dos Santos

The armed struggle was launched on 25 September 1964.

The Portuguese army was expecting an attack, but had under-estimated both our capacity and our aims. It supposed that our strategy would be based on continual harassment of Portuguese forces over the frontier, with the aim of putting pressure on the Portuguese authorities to reach a settlement. In other words, FRELIMO, protected by the 'sanctuary' of Tanzania, would be content with a series of hit-and-run raids across the border. To guard against such action, the Portuguese army had deployed a large force along the bank of the Rovuma and had evacuated the population living on the frontier.

FRELIMO, however, had prepared not for harassing action but for a full-scale people's war against the Portuguese Armed Forces, a war which would eventually lead to the defeat or sur-render of the Portuguese. This underestimation of our intent was certainly beneficial to us in the early stages of the war.

The Central Committee had instructed FRELIMO forces to mount simultaneous operations in various parts of the country, all in the interior. They were not going to 'invade' the country, as the Portuguese expected, but were, indeed, already there, reconnoitring the Portuguese positions and gathering new recruits.

They launched a number of actions on 25 September, attacking a series of administrative and military posts in Cabo Delgado Province. By November the struggle was extending to the provinces of Niassa, Zambézia and Tete, forcing the Portuguese to disperse their troops and preventing the possibility of an effective or sustained counter-attack. Facing action in four provinces at once, the Portuguese army was not in a position to mount offensive expeditions without leaving other vital positions undermanned. As a result, FRELIMO was able to consolidate its strategic position in Niassa and Cabo Delgado, which had been the objective of this first phase of the war. The units operating in Zambézia and Tete were then withdrawn and provisionally regrouped in Niassa and Cabo Delgado, to increase the offensive capacity of FRELIMO and to ensure that the gains made in these provinces would be maintained and a firm interior base for political and military action established. The Portuguese, on the other hand, could not withdraw their forces from Tete and Zambézia, as in doing so they would run the risk of facing a new offensive in these areas. In this way the enemy was compelled to keep large forces immobilized, while all FRELIMO forces could be used in action.

The success of these first operations opened the way for us to intensify recruitment and improve our organization. On 25 September 1964, FRELIMO had only 250 men trained and equipped, who operated in small units of from ten to fifteen each. Towards the middle of 1965, FRELIMO forces were already operating with units of company strength, and in 1966 the companies were organized into battalions. By 1967 the FRELIMO army had reached a strength of 8,000 men trained and equipped, not counting the people's militias or the trained recruits who were not yet armed. In other words, FRELIMO increased its fighting strength thirty-two times over in three years.

On the Portuguese side, constant increases in the size of the army and in the military budget are evidence of the impact that the war has already had. In 1964 there were some 35,000 Portuguese soldiers in Mozambique; by the end of 1967, there were from 65,000 to 70,000. In the middle of 1967, the National Assembly in Lisbon passed a law lowering the age of conscription to eighteen, and extending military service to three years, or even four in 'special cases'. Early in 1968 it was announced that even those previously considered unfit for military service, like the deaf, the mute, the crippled, would be mobilized for the auxiliary services, and that women, too, could be accepted into these.

In 1963, total military expenditure for Portugal and the colonies together was \$193 million. In 1967, for the defence of the overseas territories alone, the budget allowed \$180 million, and in April 1968 this was officially raised by \$37 million, making an expenditure of \$217 million on the colonial wars. These are the official figures provided by Lisbon, and since Portugal has good reason to underplay her military expenditure for the benefit of both world opinion and home consumption, it would not be over-rash to suppose that Portugal may now be spending something like £1 million a day to 'defend the people of the overseas provinces' from – the people of the overseas provinces.

This 'escalation' of Portuguese aggression corresponds to an increase in Portuguese losses. Compare, for example, the losses that they sustained in the first two months, January and February, of the years 1965, 1966 and 1967:

	1965	1966	1967
Soldiers killed	258	360	626

The Portuguese naturally set their losses at a much lower figure than the FRELIMO estimates, and in comparing the two sets of figures a number of considerations should be taken into account. First of all, in dealing with their own losses, the Portuguese always attribute a surprising number of deaths to 'accidents';* they spread out the announcement of casualties over a longer period of time than that in which they actually occurred; and they omit deaths of African puppet soldiers. In assessing FRELIMO losses, however, they count all Africans killed, and therefore always include a large number of civilian 'suspects'. This is apart from any direct falsification which may take place. On the other side, when FRELIMO assesses the number of Portuguese killed, it is often able to estimate only from the number which fall,

* Stanley Meisler an American journalist, was a witness to one such case of falsification.

without being able to check the bodies afterwards, and so wounded may often be counted as killed.

The Portuguese official estimate of losses to date given in mid-1967 was 378 soldiers dead – 212 killed in action and 166 as a result of 'accidents and disease' – and 3,500 wounded. Judging from their monthly reports, however, to have reached a figure as low as this they must have covered a period considerably shorter than that from the beginning of the war. Yet, even with these major discrepancies, the Portuguese figures confirm that Portuguese losses have been increasing as the war progresses. SIFA (Portuguese Army Information Services) announced over the first three days of 1968 that thirteen Portuguese soldiers had been killed in Mozambique, an officer included.

A number of factors have contributed to the success of FRELIMO forces against the much larger and better equipped Portuguese army.

On the military front, the Portuguese face all the problems of a regular army combating a guerrilla force and a foreign army of occupation fighting in hostile territory. First of all, only a small fraction of the armed forces can be used in action. The colonial government must employ large numbers to protect towns, economic interests, lines of communication, and to guard the population confined in 'protected villages'. Thus, out of the 65,000 Portuguese soldiers in Mozambique, only about 30,000 are used against our forces in Niassa and Cabo Delgado; and not even all of these are free to engage in action against us, since many are pinned down defending strategic points and population centres in the area. Secondly, the Portuguese are fighting on unfamiliar terrain against an enemy which belongs to that terrain and knows it well. Much of the land in these northern provinces is heavily wooded, providing good cover for the guerrillas and their bases. Often the only means of penetrating the bush is along narrow footpaths, where a body of men must walk in single file, a sitting target for ambush. In such conditions, heavy equipment like aircraft and armoured vehicles is of little use.

The political aspect is of even greater importance, for the struggle is essentially a political struggle in which the military is only one aspect. To justify their presence, the Portuguese must affirm that their army is defending Mozambique against outside aggression. Yet such a posture is impossible to maintain persuasively, for the FRELIMO forces are, without exception, composed of Mozambicans, whereas the Portuguese army is almost entirely composed of Portuguese troops and numbers little more than one thousand puppet African soldiers among its ranks. When it does use African troops, these are surrounded by Portuguese soldiers to guard against desertion.

Then the people themselves are in the overwhelming main hostile to the Portuguese. To prevent them cooperating with FRELIMO, the Portuguese army organizes them into 'protected villages', villages surrounded by barbed wire and guarded by Portuguese troops, the counterpart of the resettlement centres set up by the French during the Algerian war, and the strategic hamlets of the Americans in Vietnam. This may temporarily cut off the villagers from FRELIMO; but it does nothing to reduce hostility to the Portuguese, and when an opportunity arises, the population of such 'protected villages' revolts.

The war is also creating internal problems for the Portuguese government. It is faced not only with the war in Mozambique but is fighting on two other fronts, Angola and Guinea Bissau. At the same time it has to keep forces of repression in São Tomé, Cabo Verde, Macau, Timor and Portugal as well, where opposition to fascism, although severely weakened by forty years of repression, has never been completely crushed. The government's resources of manpower and money are being stretched to breaking point by wars thousands of miles from home, wars for which the population is paying but from which, for the most part, it cannot hope to gain anything. This adds fuel to internal opposition and at the same time weakens the government's defences against it. To try to fill the military gap left at home by the departure of large numbers of troops overseas, the government has invited the West Germans to establish military bases in Portugal, one of which has already been constructed at Beja and houses 1,500 German soldiers. Such a measure may strengthen the military position of the government, but weakens it politically by introducing a foreign military force to help uphold it against its own people.

The government of Portugal is not a popular government; it was established and has been maintained by force, by the army and the secret police. Yet it demands increasing sacrifices from the people. It is true that some Portuguese are able to profit immensely from the war, and the families of soldiers on active service in the colonies receive a small financial subsidy. But the price in blood is steadily growing. In 1961 500 Portuguese soldiers were killed in Angola. In the first three years of the war in Mozambique alone, the Portuguese admit to a total of nearly 4,000 killed and wounded, while the FRELIMO estimate puts this at more like 9,000. In 1967 on all three fronts about 10,000 were killed or wounded.

The effect on the population can be judged by the fact that the government has found it necessary to introduce a law forbidding all Portuguese males over the age of sixteen to leave the country without authorization from the military. Within the army itself there is more evidence to indicate the low state of morale. In 1966 it was estimated in Portugal that, since the start of the colonial wars, there had been 7,000 cases of desertion and insubordination in the army. In Mozambique a number of Portuguese soldiers have deserted directly to FRELIMO forces. Some of them were prompted mainly by the fear and discomfort suffered in the colonial army and by the treatment they received from superiors, but some deserted because of their fundamental opposition to the Salazar régime and to the war. One, Afonso Henriques Sacramento do Rio, gave his reasons:

> On the one hand, because I disagree with the régime of the dictator Salazar; on the other hand, because I did not obey orders commanding me to burn houses, massacre the Mozambican population and destroy the crops.

Another, José Inácio Bispo Catarino, gave a telling account of conditions in the Portuguese army to *Mozambique Revolution*, revealing not only why some soldiers do desert, but also why more do not; because of their ignorance about the war, about FRELIMO, and the severe surveillance of the officers:

> Our officers never tell us anything about the war. I never knew directly that we were fighting FRELIMO troops. I was aware of

143

what FRELIMO was because I used to listen secretly to Radio Moscow. I knew that FRELIMO guerrillas had killed many Portuguese troops, and I knew it was true because I could see many of my colleagues being killed. . . . I deserted because we, the Portuguese, took by force the land that belongs to the Africans. Now the owners want their land. Why should we fight against them? I cannot fight on the side of the Portuguese, because I know that what they are doing is wrong. I saw many of my companions being killed; my sergeant died in front of me, and many others; all of them died for a cause which is not theirs. I often spoke to my soldiers, telling them that they should pretend to be sick so as to be evacuated to Nampula. I organized meetings with some of the ones I trusted, and explained to them that we were suffering for a cause which was not ours. I gave them the example of our sergeant who died for nothing. We met anywhere, when we were sure of not being heard – even in bathrooms. (Interview in *Mozambique Revolution*.)

If relatively few actually desert from active service – it takes a certain level of political consciousness and determination to desert under such conditions – many do their best to avoid combat. Deserters have told us that frequently when soldiers are sent out to look for FRELIMO, they simply hide in the bush for a time and then return to camp with some suitable story made up for their superior officers. There have also been cases where companies openly refused to go on patrol in a region where FRELIMO was known to be strong. The observations of the population and of our troops confirm such stories.

Portugal looks for help from her allies to overcome her many problems, but even in this she is hindered by the conditions and nature of the war. Assistance comes mainly from NATO countries and from South Africa. The United Nations, however, has condemned Portugal's policy and criticized NATO and other countries for assisting her; moreover, there is a substantial body of opinion within the other NATO countries which is opposed to the wars of repression conducted by Portugal. As a result, the United States and Western Europe are forced to keep at a certain distance. Portugal does gain, financially and in armaments and training facilities, from the NATO alliance, not least through the experience of countries like France, Britain and the

United States in guerrilla warfare. Military assistance, however, must be in the guise of fulfilling Portugal's requirements as a member of NATO, and officially should not be used in Africa, outside the NATO area. Although some NATO armaments are certainly used in the colonies, Portugal's main gain from NATO is that her military requirements at home are largely taken care of, leaving her free to use her own resources in the colonies. While these are still inadequate, it would be politically difficult for any of her NATO allies directly to enter the colonial struggle by sending troops for use by Portugal in Africa.

South Africa, on the other hand, is relatively impervious to world opinion and makes no pretence of permitting democratic opposition within her territory. Her ability to assist Portugal, however, is limited by her own problems. She already has a large army and police force occupied in maintaining her own white régime against the indigenous movement of liberation. In addition, she is openly sending troops and arms to Rhodesia, and her commitments there are likely to grow. Traditional ties between white South Africa and the Portuguese are much less close than those between the white South Africans and the white Rhodesians, and a major involvement in the Portuguese wars would only put an added strain on her army without arousing much enthusiasm from the white population.

The same conditions which make the war difficult for Portugal act to help FRELIMO.

Because the Portuguese troops are tied down in defending various settled strategic positions, the guerrilla forces always have the initiative in choosing the time and place to mount an attack. FRELIMO forces are fighting on their own ground, in a terrain they know, among a people who know and support them. A defeat for the Portuguese means that the struggle is pushed into a new area, and that as a result they have to bring up more combat troops there, weakening still further their overall position. A defeat for FRELIMO is more easily retrievable, as it involves only a temporary reduction of strength in one area.

Any progress in the war means very much more to FRELIMO than a mere gain in territory. The war has altered the whole internal structure of the areas deeply affected by it: in the liberated zones, the various systems of exploitation have been abolished, the heavy taxes have gone, the repressive administration has been destroyed; the people are free to cultivate their land as they need to, campaigns against illiteracy have been started, schools and health services have been established, and the people are involved in political debate, in making their own decisions. However embryonic these developments may be, the change has been felt in some way or another by almost all those living in the zones, and given them that much more reason to fight. Each zone freed in this way is a reservoir of new recruits for the fighting forces. In the villages popular militias are formed which at once confirm the power of the people and relieve the ordinary FRELIMO forces of many defence tasks; by cooperation with the army, they also extend FRELIMO's overall offensive capacity.

The FRELIMO army and the population are closely linked; the people are a constant source of information and supply for FRELIMO, while they are a further source of danger to the Portuguese. FRELIMO's forces live for the most part off what they produce in the fighting areas, and what has to be transported is taken on foot through the bush between the small centres which have been established. As a result, FRELIMO has no vulnerable supply lines, no military or economic strategic positions to defend. The loss of a single small base or area of crops is not very serious; it has no significance beyond the immediate loss of resources.

The longer that the struggle lasts, the more evident becomes its popular basis, the more support flows to FRELIMO, and the more confidence there is in FRELIMO's ability to succeed, while the less confidence the allies of Portugal have in her own prospects. As the struggle progresses, material aid for FRELIMO increases, while FRELIMO becomes itself more formidable. Thus every victory adds to our chances of winning yet further victories and reduces the ability of the Portuguese to counter our activities.

The character of the FRELIMO forces

To understand the real nature of the war, it is not enough to take into account these general factors, common as they are to nearly all popular guerrilla wars. More detailed points about the composition, organization and leadership of the army are important.

The army is representative of the population at large, in that the vast majority of the guerrillas are peasants initially uneducated, illiterate and often unable to speak any Portuguese; but there is also a scattering of those who have had some education within the Portuguese system. The majority naturally come from the areas at present affected by the fighting, because it is there that widespread campaigns of political education and training programmes are possible. There is, however, a continual stream of people from further south, from all over Mozambique, who escape in order to join the struggle; and at the beginning, many people from refugee camps, who had fled from every district of Mozambique to escape repression, joined as soon as a structure to contain them had been created. In the army, people from different areas accordingly mingle, so that each unit contains representatives from different tribes and different areas fighting together. In this way, tribalism is being effectively combated within the forces, and an example is being set to the rest of the population.

This is not the only way in which the army leads the way to social change. By accepting women into its ranks, it has revolutionized their social position. Women now play a very active part in running popular militias, and there are also many guerrilla units composed of women. Through the army, women have started to take responsibility in many areas; they have learned to stand up and speak at public meetings, to take an active part in politics. In fact they do a great deal of important work in mobilizing the population. When a women's unit first visits a village which is not yet sufficiently involved with FRELIMO, the sight of armed women who get up and talk in front of a large audience causes great amazement, even incredulity; when the villagers are convinced that the soldiers in front of them really are women, the effect on the astonished men is often so forceful that the rush of recruits is very much greater than the army can cope with or than the area can afford to lose.

The army is helping to raise the standard of education as well as of general political consciousness. Recruits are taught wherever possible to read and write, and to speak Portuguese, and even where an organized teaching programme cannot be arranged, they are encouraged to help each other to learn these basic skills. Indeed, the Portuguese authorities are increasingly suspicious of ordinary peasants who speak Portuguese, because they know that these are more likely to have learned it in the FRELIMO army than in a Portuguese school. The army also organizes various specific training programmes such as radio work, accounting, typing, as well as in subjects more narrowly orientated to the war. Finally, the army cultivates and produces its own food wherever possible, thereby relieving the population of the burden of supporting it and at the same time spreading the lessons of its example.

In these respects the army leads the people; but more important yet is the fact that the army is the people, and it is the people who form the army. There are civilian members of FRELIMO engaged in all types of work among the population; but cooperation extends beyond this, to the large body of peasants who are not members of FRELIMO, but who support the struggle, looking to the army for protection and the party for assistance of various kinds. They in turn help the militants whenever they can.

These features are best substantiated from the words of the militants themselves:

Joaquim Maquival, from Zambézia: I come from Zambézia, a Chuabo, and I have fought in Niassa where the people are Nyanjas, and they received me like a son. I have worked among Ajuas, Macuas, who received me as if I were their own son. (F.I.)

Miguel Ambrósio, company commander from Cabo Delgado: I have fought in Zambézia and Niassa, far from my own region and my own tribe. I have fought in the country of the Chuabos and the Lomes. . . . The Chuabos, the Nyanjas and the Lomes received me even more warmly than if I had been from their own region. In Western Niassa, for example, I came across Comrade Panguene, and although he is from the south, you couldn't distinguish him from the people of the region: he is like a son of the region. The people understand that we are all Mozambicans. . . . The people are united and help us. Otherwise, for instance, we couldn't go into enemy areas; it is the people who give us all our information about the movements of the enemy, their strength and their position. Also, when we start working in an area where we have no food, because we have not yet had the opportunity to grow any, the people supply us and feed us. We also help the people. Until militias have been formed in a region, we protect the people in their fields against the action and reprisals of the colonialists; we organize new villages when we have to evacuate the people from a zone because of the war; we protect them against the enemy. (F.I.)

Rita Mulumbua, woman militant from Niassa: In our units there are people from every region; I am with Ajuas, Nyanjas, Makondes, and people from Zambézia. I believe this is good; before we did not think of ourselves as a single nation; FRELIMO has shown us that we are one people. We have united to destroy Portuguese colonialism and imperialism.

The struggle has transformed us. FRELIMO gave me the chance to study. The colonialists didn't want us to study, while now I am in this detachment we train in the morning and in the afternoon I go to school to learn reading and writing. The Portuguese didn't want us to study, because if we did we would understand, we would know things. For this reason FRELIMO wants us to study so that we should know, and in knowing we understand better, we fight better and will serve our country better. (F.I.)

Natacha Deolinda, woman militant from Manica and Sofala: When I went into the army, FRELIMO put me through a course on youth organization and also gave me my military training. Then I went to work in Cabo Delgado province. Our detachment held meetings everywhere explaining the politics of our party, the reasons for the struggle and also the role of the Mozambican woman in the revolution.

The Mozambican woman participates in all revolutionary activities; she helps the combatants, she has an important role in production, she grows crops, she also has military training and fights, she joins the militias which protect the people and the fields. (F.I.)

It is clear from these comments that the role of the army goes far beyond simply fighting the Portuguese. Like the party, it is a nation-making force. It prepares not just soldiers but future citizens, who pass on what they learn to the people among whom they work.

Leadership is not based on rank but on the concept of responsibility; the leader of a certain body is referred to as the man 'responsible' for it. Many of those now 'responsible' had never been to school before they entered the army; they were illiterate, with no formal education, when they joined near the beginning of the war. They have acquired the ability to lead through their practical experience of fighting and political work, and through the education programmes of the army. There were some who had had a little schooling; but very few of these, even among those in the most important positions today, had gone beyond primary school.

Our experience, that of the militants and the leaders, has developed with the struggle. In 1964 the army comprised small groups of men, frequently ill-armed and ill-supplied, able to mount only ambushes and small-scale raids. The army was fighting against tremendous odds. The following account, by a man who is now national political commissar and a member of the Central Committee, gives some indication of what the war was like at the beginning, of the people who engaged in it, and of how they were able to expand their activities. Some of this man's earlier struggle with the Portuguese educational and economic structure have been related in previous chapters. The present account begins just after he was forced to flee from Mozambique.

Raul Casal Ribeiro: Some comrades from FRELIMO found me and educated me. ... Three months later I asked to join FRELIMO. From then on I was a member of FRELIMO and began to work. I went to one of our party's bases to do my training, and since then I have been fighting. We have had to face many difficulties. There were times at the beginning when we didn't even have food. There were moments of hesitation, but the work of political education had taught me how to accept sacrifices and to struggle on.

The party had confidence in me and gave me responsibility. I studied hard. I was entrusted with the education of other comrades in the units. Then I was put in charge of sabotage on the Tete-Maturara railway line and other operations. We had a tiny detachment and very little equipment; the enemy sent a whole battalion to destroy us, but they failed. They attacked us, but they always suffered major losses. On one occasion they encircled us when we had only five bullets between us. They fired on us, but we had taken cover. Thinking that they had killed us, since we had not answered their fire, they advanced. When they came to within three or four metres of us, the comrades who had the bullets opened fire and killed one of them. The Portuguese were frightened and withdrew, giving us the opportunity to escape without them knowing. From a distance they went on firing for an hour, even shooting at each other. Afterwards we found the body of a South African Boer who had been with the Portuguese and had been killed by them.

This is how the enemy sows the wind and reaps the whirlwind. In this battle we captured one MG 3, six loaded magazines, one offensive and two defensive grenades, and a knife. (F.I.)

It was through such small operations with courage and initiative in the face of difficult conditions, that the present size and strength of the army became possible. As an indication of the rapid growth of guerrilla action, here is a communiqué relating to an action which took place on 2 August 1967 and which was subsequently confirmed by a report on the Portuguese radio:

Three aircraft and a store of ammunition completely destroyed; the fuel deposit burnt; nearly all houses near the airfield ruined; dozens of Portuguese soldiers killed or wounded: this happened at Mueda in a mortar attack launched by FRELIMO forces on 2 August. The fire raged for two days. (FRELIMO communiqué)

The organization of the army

After fighting began, the army was enlarged dramatically with new recruits from the areas of action; and in order to use this growing force efficiently, the organization had to be rapidly improved. The army itself was organized into battalions subdivided into detachments, companies and units. This has meant that, while small-scale operations can still be carried on over a very wide area of country, we also have available much larger forces for more important actions, such as attacks on Portuguese posts or against the Mueda air-base.

The system of leadership also had to be adjusted to meet the changing conditions of the war. Initially, the fighting areas were divided into military regions, each with a regional command; but during the first two years of the war, there was no central command outside the Department of Defence and Security, headed by a secretary just like any other department of the organization. The secretary dealt with all the details of military work, and although from time to time he would delegate his authority to one or other of his army colleagues, there was no fixed division of responsibility. The system worked reasonably well while the guerrilla forces were very small, and their action weak and limited; but as soon as the number of guerrillas in action increased, and the fighting regions expanded, a more elaborate system was required. This had to be based on an effective central command, for in the first years of fighting we found that, without a central authority, it is impossible to coordinate and supply the various forces that operate in distant parts of the country.

At a meeting of the Central Committee in 1966, therefore, it was decided that the army should be reorganized, with a high command which would operate from a settled headquarters. This decision led to the formation of the National Commanding Council, which is now headed by the Secretary for the Department of Defence (D.D.); his assistant, who is Political Commissar of the army; and twelve other leaders responsible for the separate sections of the army. The army was divided into twelve sections: (1) operations; (2) recruitment, the training and formation of cadres; (3) logistics (supplies); (4) reconnaissance; (5) transmission and communication; (6) information and military publications (which also edits the duplicated journal *25 de setembro*, written by FRELIMO militants); (7) administration; (8) finance; (9) health; (10) political commissariat; (11) personnel; and (12) military security.

Thus the army now has its own system of national administration, on the same lines as the civilian administration and parallel to it. On the local level also, the army now has a clearly defined structure. In each province there is (1) a provincial chief, who is also the under-secretary of the province; (2) an assistant provincial chief; (3) a political commissar; (4) an operational chief.

By this new method of organization, each leader has a clearly defined area of responsibility in which he must use his initiative, but also has an established channel of contact with the high command. It was put into effect at the beginning of 1967, and almost immediately things began to work more efficiently: communications from the provinces began to reach headquarters with greater regularity; arms and equipment began to flow out more rapidly to the fighting areas; recruitment increased; and plans for new and more extensive campaigns against the enemy became operational.

In a situation like this, where a country is in a state of war and the army inevitably has very extensive powers, there is a potential danger of conflict between the military and civilian organizations. In our system, though, this is minimized by the fact that they are both answerable to the political body of FRELIMO, which is itself composed both of military and civilian personnel. The relationship of the political, military and civilian bodies is not one which can be described in terms of a neat hierarchy, where one is subordinated to another. Policy decisions are made by the political body, the supreme organ of which is the Central Committee. The army, like the various departments, works in conformity with the decisions made by the Central Committee; but the army leaders themselves, as members of the Central Committee, also help to make these policy decisions. The meetings of the military command, which take place once a fortnight, are normally presided over by the President or Vice-President of FRELIMO, which ensures that between Central Committee meetings, close coordination of political and military decisions is maintained.

On the local level, in the field, the people's militia plays an important part in linking the civilian population and the army. These militias are formed from militant members of the civilian population, who carry on with their normal occupations and, at the same time, though not incorporated in the guerrilla army, undertake certain military duties. Their main task is the defence of their home region. If there is a danger of attack from the

Portuguese forces, they can be mobilized as an additional armed force. While there is fighting in an area, they coordinate their activities with the guerrillas, reinforce them when necessary, and supply them with information about the particular locality. When the guerrilla forces have liberated an area, the militia can then take over the organization of defence, of production and supply, leaving the main forces free to move on to a new fighting area. In regions where there is not yet an active armed struggle, militias are formed in secret whose task is to prepare the ground for guerrilla fighting; to mobilize the people; to observe the Portuguese forces; to arrange supplies and assistance for the guerrillas as they move into the region.

In a sense, these people's militias are the backbone of the armed struggle. The guerrillas carry the main offensives and do most of the direct fighting, but it is the work of the militias which makes it possible for them to operate.

The development of the struggle

After the initial phase of our offensive was over and our forces had withdrawn to the two northern provinces, there followed a period of apparent stalemate which lasted through 1965 and most of 1966. During this period, FRELIMO controlled most of the country and villages in the northern area; the Portuguese controlled the towns and retained a number of fortified bases where they were relatively secure. The main roads were disputed, as the Portuguese were still trying to use them for the transport of soldiers and supplies, while FRELIMO was constantly mining them and mounting ambushes. The Portuguese were unable to mount an effective offensive because, when they left their bases and went into the bush to look for our forces, they were ambushed. On the other hand, FRELIMO was not yet strong enough to mount major attacks against the Portuguese positions. Yet all the while FRELIMO was gaining strength, consolidating the military and political position, training new recruits, and gradually eroding the Portuguese strength in many small actions.

By the second half of 1966, the increased strength of
FRELIMO was becoming apparent, and our forces were able
to begin assailing the Portuguese bases themselves. Between
September 1966 and August 1967, more than thirty Portuguese
military bases were attacked; and at least ten more in the last
three months of 1967. Many of these bases were badly damaged,
and some were evacuated after the attacks. For example, the
post of Maniamba (Western Niassa) was attacked on 15 August
and evacuated; it was reoccupied, but abandoned again after a
second attack on 31 August; ten days after this a strong body of
marines was sent to reoccupy it. On 13 September, the post of
Nambude (Cabo Delgado) was attacked, and buildings, three
vehicles and the radio equipment were destroyed. The airforce
base at Mueda, an extremely important target and heavily
guarded by the Portuguese, was bombarded twice, and five
planes were completely destroyed on the ground there.

During 1967 the area of fighting was extended in all regions.
In Cabo Delgado our forces advanced to the river Lúrio and
surrounded Porto Amelia, the capital, at the same time consolidating their position in the rest of the province, which is now almost entirely in our hands. In Niassa, our forces have advanced
to the Marrupa-Maua line, and are approaching the frontiers of
the provinces of Mozambique and Zambézia. To the south, they
have gained control of Catur zone, between the provinces of
Zambézia and Tete; while, to the west, they created the conditions necessary for reopening the struggle in Tete and Zambézia,
a region of great importance for its agricultural and mineral
resources.

The Portuguese have been working to improve their anti-
guerrilla tactics and in particular have been trying to profit
from the experience of their NATO allies: Britain in Malaya,
the United States in Vietnam, and France in Algeria. Afonso
Henriques Sacramento do Rio reported:

This instruction is given to the Portuguese soldiers in the first part
of their six months' training. The soldiers learned the theoretical base
of anti-guerrilla warfare in courses tested by examinations. These
courses are usually given by officers who have undergone special
training, theoretical and practical. During the Algerian war, several

Portuguese officers were given military training in Algeria by French specialists in 'subversive warfare'. Many other officers have been sent to the USA, where they took commando and marine courses and studied all the techniques used by the American army against the Vietnamese people.

One effect of this is that the Portuguese army now rarely operates in units below company strength, so that when these units are attacked, even if they suffer heavy losses, they retain a sufficient numerical strength to prevent the guerrillas from achieving one of their chief objectives: the capture of arms and ammunition.

None the less, the Portuguese are still suffering heavy losses when they attempt to leave their bases, and are making little headway against the guerrilla forces, who simply retreat until such time as they can attack with advantage. As a result, the Portuguese have been turning more and more to aerial warfare, knowing that it is not easy for us to acquire and transport the type of heavy equipment needed against such action. They have carried out raids against bases, villages, schools, clinics; bombed areas of crops, and made some attempts in places to destroy the bush which gives cover to our guerrillas. The casualties caused by these raids have been almost entirely among the civilian population, and high priority has been given by us to organizing protection for the villagers. We are increasing our anti-aircraft strength; in October 1967 one of three planes which were bombing Marrupa zone was shot down, and the others were forced to withdraw.

Faced with a series of military reverses, the Portuguese authorities have been experimenting with various extra-military anti-guerrilla tactics, a mixture of terrorism and psychological warfare, with the main aim of forcing or persuading the population to withdraw support from FRELIMO. On the psychological side, in 1966 and 1967 they mounted propaganda campaigns on the radio and through a wide-scale distribution of leaflets. These leaflets were in general attractively printed on brightly coloured paper, with a parallel text in Portuguese and an African language, describing conditions of starvation and misery in FRELIMO areas, and of a prosperous, comfortable life under the Portuguese. They carried large pictures illustrating this contrast or caricaturing FRELIMO as 'living it up' in exile at the expense of the rest of the population. In their propaganda they have also tried to exploit natural divisions in the population, accusing FRELIMO of fostering one tribe's ambitions against its neighbour.

The distance between the Portuguese and the African population, however, greatly diminishes the effect of such campaigns, since with the high level of illiteracy and the low material standards prevailing, pamphlets and radio cannot by themselves reach a wide audience. Besides this, the falsity of the content is not hard to see; the people remember well enough that there was no prosperity under the Portuguese, and where FRELIMO has been active they will have observed themselves that its members and leaders are drawn from different tribes and different religious groups. FRELIMO has the vast advantage that its political work is carried out mostly through personal contact, by word of mouth, by meetings, by example, and is convincingly undertaken by members of the ordinary population. Moreover, there is no attempt to distort the truth by promising impossibilities: we admit that the war may be long; that it will certainly be difficult; that it will not bring prosperity and happiness by magic; but that it is bringing some improvements and that it is the only way of eventually achieving a better life. The message issued to the Mozambican people from the Central Committee on 25 September 1967, for example, stated:

... There are many difficulties. The guerrillas sometimes have to spend whole days without eating, have to sleep out in the cold, and sometimes have to march days or even weeks in order to carry out an attack or an ambush. ... The people also suffer in this stage of the liberation struggle, for the enemy intensifies its repression to try to terrorize the population and prevent them from supporting the guerrillas. There are many difficulties. The battle for liberty is not easy. But that liberty we want to gain is worth all these sacrifices ...

The work of mobilization is done essentially through direct contact, but it is backed up by literature and by the radio. Statements and messages such as the one quoted above are duplicated and distributed in the camps and at meetings. Simple duplicated leaflets are also circulated, depicting, for example, an exploiting 'boss' being driven out by FRELIMO. There are also regular broadcasts, organized through Radio Tanzania, which, since 1967, have been powerful enough to reach beyond the southern border of Mozambique. In the liberated areas, we have distributed radio sets to help the people hear these broadcasts. Programmes include: news in Portuguese and African languages; reports on the struggle; messages and political talks; educational programmes on hygiene and public health; revolutionary songs, traditional and popular music.

Having obtained very little result from direct propaganda, the Portuguese have been trying to develop more elaborate techniques. In 1967, for example, they set up a puppet African in Tete Province as leader of a 'nationalist' party and arranged public meetings where he appeared with Portuguese officials and asserted that the Portuguese were prepared to grant independence peacefully to his party but not to the 'FRELIMO bandits'. This campaign had some initial success; but as explanations from FRELIMO militants were backed up by a lack of any signs of good faith on the part of the Portuguese, the people became sceptical and for the most part stopped going to the meetings.

Faced with the failure of both military action and 'persuasion', the Portuguese have been relying increasingly on terror, in an attempt to frighten away support from FRELIMO. Seeing the liberation forces living among the people like fish in the water, they want to heat the water until it cooks the fish.

Since the war, all over Mozambique, and not just within the fighting areas, there have been drives to round up nationalist sympathizers, and thousands of 'suspects' have been arrested. The majority of these are peasants and manual workers, 'natives' by Portuguese terminology. They are not brought to trial, nor sentenced; they are imprisoned, interrogated, tortured and not seldom executed in complete secrecy. Even their families are not told anything definite: all they know is that the person disappears.

Among these 'suspects' there have also been a few intellectuals, people too well known beyond Mozambique to be allowed simply to vanish without causing an international outcry. Such have included the poets José Craveirinha and Rui Nogar; Malangatana Valente, the painter; Luis Bernardo Honwana, the short story writer. The Portuguese authorities brought just these few prominent men to trial, making their case public and trying to give the impression that all their proceedings against nationalists, saboteurs, etc., were conducted in the same open legal manner. But even such a show trial did not conform to the standards of legality laid down in non-fascist countries. When it first took place in March 1966, as many as nine of the thirteen accused were acquitted for lack of evidence; but the government refused to accept this verdict and ordered a new trial by military tribunal. This tribunal, acting under precise government instructions, convicted those who had been acquitted before and lengthened the sentences imposed on the other four. The sentences themselves are in any case meaningless, because they all included 'security measures', which mean that the term of imprisonment can be extended indefinitely. A delegation of international jurists and all foreign journalists were forbidden to attend this second trial.

Yet the Portuguese succeeded to some extent in their intentions, for the international outcry directed specifically against this trial and the fate of those thirteen intellectuals helped to draw attention away from the real issue: the much worse fate of the many undistinguished Mozambicans who have not been given even the semblance of a trial, but have been either killed or else imprisoned under very much more severe conditions.

In the fighting areas, the campaign of terror is more widespread, and more indiscriminate, with reprisals carried out against the population as a whole. Where it cannot reach the villages, the Portuguese army resorts to air-raids, but where the soldiers are able to get to the people, more personal forms of terror and torture are used. The type of incident will be only too familiar to anyone who has studied the methods of fascist armies elsewhere.

Extreme brutality, however, does not as a rule have the desired result but confirms the people in their hostility to the Portuguese, and in fact often drives them to desperate acts of defiance.

Such a policy is thus not only cruel; it is tactically foolish. The FRELIMO army, in contrast, is firmly and constantly instructed to attack military and economic targets. The statements of militants indicate how they understand this policy.

Joaquim Maquival: ... In our units and on our missions we have often come across unarmed Portuguese civilians. We didn't harm them. We asked where they were coming from; we explained our struggle to them, our sufferings; we received them kindly. We do this because our struggle, our war, is not against the Portuguese people; we are struggling against the Portuguese government, against those who turn their weapons on the Mozambican people; we are at war with those who injure the people. ... We know that it is not all the people of Portugal who exploit us, but only a minority, which is also exploiting the Portuguese people themselves. Among the Portuguese people there are also people who are exploited. FRELIMO cannot fight the people, cannot fight against the exploited.

Miguel Ambrósio Cunumoshuvi (company commander): We have never thought of murdering Portuguese civilians; we don't terrorize the Portuguese civilian population because we know who we are fighting and why. For that reason, we have never planned an attack against Portuguese civilians. If we wanted to, we could; the civilians live near us, we have every opportunity; but our objective, our target is the army, the police, the administration.

Our programme, our standing orders state clearly that we must not attack any civilian, only those people who are with the army, that is, accompanying and assisting it. The only terrorists in Mozambique are the colonialists.

This policy has importance for the future, when we shall be trying to establish a society that can absorb the different people living in Mozambique without racial bitterness; but it also has immediate practical advantages. At the beginning of the war, for instance, the Portuguese authorities distributed arms to the white *colonatos* and traders in certain areas for use against FRELIMO. These people then saw that unarmed civilians would not be harmed, but that those who carried arms against us would be treated as an appendage of the army; and the result was that most of the civilians refused to accept arms. The failure of the Portuguese forces to understand this policy has even sometimes roused the Portuguese civilians against them: in one instance the Portuguese forces entered a village where they knew that FRELIMO had been, and when they found that the Portuguese civilians had not been touched, they accused them of collaborating with FRELIMO and arrested and punished them, their own settlers.

Tete and the new offensive

When FRELIMO military forces withdrew from Tete Province after the first phase of the war, underground workers remained to conduct political mobilization and prepare for the time when this front would be reopened. By the end of 1967, when the gains made in Cabo Delgado and Niassa had been consolidated and our forces in those two provinces were pushing south, conditions were created for the extension of the war into Tete. At last, in March 1968, the first military operations began.

This new phase of the war is particularly important, because of the military and economic plans which the Portuguese had made for this area. Tete is a key region of Mozambique: the great Zambezi river passes through the centre of it; the province contains considerable economic resources and is crossed by important lines of communication, including the main road from Salisbury to Blantyre; on a north-south axis it lies roughly in the centre of the country.

The Portuguese had originally planned two lines of defence. The first was the Nacala-Maniamba line, which our troops broke through when they extended operations to Macanhelas in the extreme south of Niassa. The second defence line is the Zambezi river. There is a heavy concentration of troops along the river, and in addition the Portuguese plan to allocate one million settlers in the valley to act as a barrier to our forces. Thus from a purely military point of view the whole length of the Zambezi valley is extremely important.

The Tete area has also acquired considerable economic significance as a result of the recent development plan associated with the Cabora Bassa dam. Tete contains some of the richest land in Mozambique, and agriculture there is fairly well developed, particularly the raising of cattle and other livestock. There are also important deposits of minerals which have as yet been very little exploited. The plan allows for the development of all these resources, largely by the proposed Portuguese settlers to be planted along the defence line. The dam itself will provide power for a variety of industries based on the products of the region, as well as water for new agricultural projects. The Cabora Bassa site is, therefore, clearly one of the most important targets in this phase of the war.

This area is also crucial in the wider context of the Southern African alliance. In the south, Tete province borders on Rhodesia, and thus the progress of our struggle here is of considerable interest to the Zimbabwan liberation forces. Of more immediate importance, however, is the involvement of South Africa herself. She is taking a large share in the expense of the dam's construction and expects to absorb a considerable proportion of the power supplied. Here in Tete, then, for the first time we are coming into conflict directly with South Africa. She is already so worried about her interests that she has sent troops to help guard the dam site. Our forces have observed one battalion of South African troops in Chioco and several companies in Chicoa, Mague and Zumbo.

The South African army is extremely well equipped with the latest Western weapons, and the presence of such troops will no doubt make the struggle much harder. But it has been clear for at least two years now that the Portuguese were anxious to obtain more direct assistance from South Africa, and we knew that eventually, as we pressed south, the threat from South Africa would increase. The fact that we are already facing South African troops is a sign of how rapidly the war has progressed; it indicates our strength and the weakness of the Portuguese.

Furthermore, the presence of the South Africans has not prevented us from taking the offensive in Tete. On 8 March we mounted several operations simultaneously: an ambush near Kassuenda village; ambushes in the zones of Furancungo, Fingue and Vila Vasco da Gama; an attack against the enemy post of Malavela. In these operations at least twelve Portuguese soldiers were killed, including a sergeant; and at Malavela four houses, a lorry and the water deposit were destroyed.

8 The New Mozambique

The purpose of our struggle is not only to destroy. It is first and foremost aimed at building a new Mozambique, where there will be no hunger and where all men will be free and equal. We are fighting with arms in our hands, because in order to build the Mozambique that we want we must first destroy the Portuguese colonial system . . . only after this will we be able to use for ourselves our labour and the wealth of our country . . .

Message from the Central Committee to the Mozambican people for 25 September 1967, the anniversary of the beginning of the struggle.

One of the chief lessons to be drawn from nearly four years of war in Mozambique is that liberation does not consist merely of driving out the Portuguese authority, but also of constructing a new country; and that this construction must be undertaken even while the colonial state is in the process of being destroyed. We realized this in principle before we began fighting, but it is only in the development of the struggle that we have learned quite how rapid and comprehensive civil reconstruction must be. There is no question of making a few provisional arrangements and waiting until we control our whole country before deciding how to govern it. We are having now to evolve structures and make decisions which will set the pattern for the future national government.

One of the first results of the war is the elimination of the colonial state where its repressive forces have disappeared. Portuguese law, administration and systems of economic exploitation leave in the wake of Portuguese arms.

On the ruins of the colonial state a new type of power is emerging which corresponds to the forces which have brought about the revolution. Before the war two authorities coexisted:

the colonial, and that of the traditional chiefdoms subordinated and integrated into the colonial system but retaining nevertheless a certain autonomy. When the colonial power is destroyed by a guerrilla victory in a given area, this leaves an administrative void. The power of tribal chiefs, however, has its origins in the traditional life of the country, and in the past was based on a popular conception of legitimacy, not on force. For the future, this therefore poses potential problems of tribalism and regionalism. In its precolonial form, such traditional government often served its purpose quite well within a limited area, providing an adequate form of organization in the interests of the majority; but even in such cases, limited in its scope and based on a small local unit, it cannot form a satisfactory foundation for the needs of a modern state. In other areas, such power already had an element of feudalism, permitting an exploitation of the peasantry which, masked by metaphysical and religious claims, was accepted. The survival of such systems is obviously a hindrance to the progress of a revolution that aims at social and political equality. The effect of colonialism, moreover, was to pervert all traditional power structures, encouraging or creating authoritarian and élitist elements.

In its session of October 1966, the Central Committee of FRELIMO re-examined the problems of tribalism and regionalism, and vigorously condemned the 'tribalist or regional tendencies shown by certain comrades in the execution of their work, reaffirming solemnly that such attitudes are contrary to the interests of the Mozambican people and impede the successful development of the people's liberation struggle. It emphasizes that the battle against tribalism and regionalism is as important as the battle against colonialism, such a battle being the safeguard of our national unity and our liberty'.

Certainly, where the chiefs have allied themselves with Portuguese power, there is little problem. *A Voz da Revolução* relates one instance:

Certain chiefs, afraid of losing their feudal privileges with the victory of the revolution and the installation of a popular government, allied themselves with the colonialists . . .

Chief Nhapale of Muturara region (Tete Province) was one of these . . .

The population reacted against him, and to mark their protest against the behaviour of the chief, went in a large body to see him. There the *régulo* was told that he would be punished and that FRELIMO would bring him to justice . . .

The leader of the FRELIMO unit then spoke to the people and to the *régulo* saying:

'*Régulo* Nhapale, we are members of FRELIMO. We have come because we have heard that you lead the people badly.' He turned to the assembled company:

'This *régulo* has had two innocent people burnt alive, two patriots. Do you want to keep such a chief?'

The people answered NO, and, encouraged by the presence of the guerrillas, put the chief through a summary trial and condemned him to death . . .

Nhapale was executed.

In other instances, where the chiefs have remained neutral or even come out positively on the side of the struggle, the progress of revolutionary power has the effect that traditional power gradually fades away. Certainly, where the traditional power does not actively uphold the colonial structure or oppose the revolution, the change has to come through positive developments, the emergence of new forms of power, of new political ideas. The main weapon in this struggle is general and political education, achieved through practical experience as well as in meetings, discussions and lessons.

The army, we have already shown, is a powerful vehicle of change. Everyone in the army lives and works with people from all over Mozambique in a completely new structure. The army can spread ideas and set an example. Here too, though, there is another potential danger, which was also discussed at the same Central Committee meeting of October 1966. In a report of this meeting, we stated:

The Central Committee also considered the attitude of comrades who think that there are two types of FRELIMO members, those in the army and those in civil life; it considered that such an attitude shows on their part a great lack of understanding of the popular, national and unitary character of the national liberation struggle which is leading the Mozambican people, and it reaffirmed that all members of

FRELIMO may be called upon – and must therefore be ready – to accomplish any task whether or not it be of a military character.

Here again the solution must lie in education and practical organization.

In the liberated areas, the political structure is the party. In the villages, people's militias are created which are dependent on the local party organization and on the military leadership of the zone; their power rests on the nationalist and revolutionary forces. Besides this, economic life is organized so that the producers work in cooperatives under the direction of the local party; this takes away from the chief his traditional role as organizer of the economic life and at the same time puts an end to the exploitation of the peasantry by any privileged group. It should also be stressed that this process is not a 'dictatorship of the party': the party is an open organization, and its members are drawn from the whole population, with the majority being, as is the majority of the population, peasants; its role is to provide a political framework above the local level. There is no deep distinction between party and population: the party is the population engaged in political action.

Public meetings, held through the local party, are an important part of life in the liberated areas. At these, non-party members can hear more about FRELIMO and about the struggle, can voice their opinions, ask questions and enter into discussion. The work of political education, the example and explanations given by the 'responsible' members and the political commissars, and the fact that the struggle is led by elements of the working masses, all go to create conditions for the disappearance of traditional tribal and often semi-feudal power and for its replacement by new forms of power. At the present time the administrative life of villages is being reorganized on the basis of people's committees elected by the whole population, and the way is being prepared for the extension of this system to the district level.

The void left by the destruction of the colonial state posed a practical problem which had not been clearly envisaged by the leadership: a series of services disappeared along with Portuguese rule, particularly services of a commercial nature, while the people continued to exist and to require such services. The inadequacy of the colonial administration meant that there were also many social needs that had never been met but which were nevertheless strongly felt by the population. Thus, from the time of the first victories in the war, a great variety of administrative responsibilities fell on FRELIMO. A population of some 800,000 had to be served. First and foremost, their material needs had to be satisfied, an adequate food supply assured, and other important articles such as clothes, soap, or matches provided; then medical and educational services had to be established, and administrative and judicial systems organized.

For a time the problem was acute. We had been unprepared for the extent of the work before us, and we lacked experience in most of the fields where we needed it. In some areas, shortages were very serious; and where the peasants did not understand the reasons, they were withdrawing their support from the struggle and in some instances leaving the region altogether. During the two years after the struggle began, the battle to build up services in the liberated areas and to educate the population was at least as important as the military one. By 1966 the crisis was past. The worst shortages had been overcome, and embryonic structures had been formed for commerce, administration, health and education. The New Mozambique was beginning to take shape.

Political structure

The emerging political structure follows the characteristic pattern of one party democracy; and FRELIMO, as well as being the driving force behind the liberation struggle, is becoming the government in the liberated areas. The essential structure of the party was formulated in 1962, at the first Congress; but since at that time there was no liberated territory and no possibility of legal political activity in Mozambique, the original pattern was orientated towards underground organization. This structure has subsequently developed to fulfil effectively the function of a legal government in the areas which have come under our control.

The Congress is the supreme organ of FRELIMO and is formed of elected representatives of the people. The delegates to the 1962 Congress, of course, were necessarily elected only by a very small minority of the population, who were in contact with the various political organizations and who were able, either by working underground, or because they were living abroad, to escape the surveillance of the secret police. The Congress elected a Central Committee of twenty members and delegated to this committee the total responsibility for directing the liberation struggle. The Central Committee, therefore, combined legislative, judicial and executive powers – a situation which began to create problems as the party grew into the large and complex organization it is now.

One of the first tasks of the Central Committee was to establish a political structure inside Mozambique. Until 1964, all activity had to be clandestine, which meant that still only a small minority of the population, the most politically advanced, could be involved. Once some areas were liberated, however, the party could come into the open there as a public legal body, with membership open to every adult Mozambican. Here, the party provides a coherent structure for mass representation.

The smallest party unit is the cell, which consists of all the members in a particular locality. At the next level is the district council, which consists of representatives elected by the members of all the cells in the district. The district council then elects representatives to the provincial council, and the provincial councils in their turn elect the delegates to the Congress. At each level, decisions are reached through discussion, and if there are irresolvable differences of opinion, the issue is decided by a vote, with the minority held to the majority decision.

As well as contributing to national policy, the local organs of the party have responsibility for local government. The exact structure of this varies from region to region, as existing para-political structures, traditional and modern, have been incorporated in the structure of the liberation movement. In areas where cooperatives have been established, the cooperative committees take over several functions of a local government body, and this system, which is spreading rapidly, is likely to become an important factor in local government of the future. Meanwhile, a variety of systems coexist, each one geared to the specific conditions prevalent in the particular locality.

At the level of the Central Committee, the work of the party both as a liberation force and as a provisional government, was organized into a number of departments. The Department of Administration took over the day-to-day problems of organization: the transportation of materials; the buying and selling, the import and export of goods: preparation and distribution of FRELIMO membership cards, and the maintenance of an up-to-date list of members; control over the movement of FRELIMO civilians, with the arrangement of food, clothes and accommodation, and the issue of money and, where necessary, travel documents.

The Department of External Affairs took responsibility for relations with foreign governments and organizations. It arranges for representatives to go abroad, to attend conferences or simply visit other countries and explain our position and discuss our problems. It is in charge of the permanent centres in Dar es Salaam, Lusaka, Algiers, Cairo and New York. It deals with questions of aid and diplomatic support from abroad.

The Department of Finance is responsible for administering the funds of the organization. The assets of the organization are derived partly from Mozambique, from membership subscriptions, donations, levies, and the proceeds of exports; partly from abroad, from donations given by foreign governments and by foreign or international organizations. From these funds, all the programmes of the party have to be financed.

The Department of Information, Publicity and Propaganda is concerned first of all with keeping the people of Mozambique informed about the work and aims of FRELIMO, about the situation in Mozambique and its context in the rest of the world; and in countering enemy propaganda campaigns. It also shares with the Department of External Affairs the task of informing the rest of the world about Mozambique and our struggle; it prepares and circulates written information, maintaining contact with the international press, libraries, academic bodies and other interested individuals and organizations.

The Department of Social Affairs was originally concerned with the refugees who had come from Mozambique to Tanzania; mainly with trying to collect and distribute to them the basic necessities of life. Once the war began, however, it extended its activities inside Mozambique, dealing with the problems of large sections of the population who had had to move their homes because of the fighting, or who had had them destroyed. In the first place, this involved supplying them with food and clothes, and trying to organize basic medical services. In the long run, though, it means helping them to resettle and build new homes; to become self-sufficient again as quickly as possible. And with the war in progress, work among the refugees outside Mozambique has been reorientated, towards persuading and helping them to return to liberated areas, to rebuild villages there and take part in the struggle.

Similarly, the Department of Education was concerned at the outset mainly with organizing courses abroad for those students who had managed to escape from Mozambique. Then, with the creation of liberated areas, its primary objective became the establishment of schools and training courses to serve the population inside the country.

The effect of the war and the progress made in the first two years after 1964 rapidly overextended the political and administrative structure set up in 1962. The party developed to meet the new circumstances; new departments were formed and the original departments expanded their activities. But some essential changes were necessary, changes which only the Congress had the power to make.

According to the party statutes, a Congress should have been called in 1965; but various problems forced us to postpone this until 1968. By then, however, the achievements of the struggle were such that it was possible to hold the Congress inside Mozambique, in a liberated area of Niassa province, and delegates were able to come from every province of the country, even from

Lourenço Marques and Gaza Province in the extreme south. The delegates to this Congress had been elected through the local party network, operating openly in the liberated areas and secretly in the areas under Portuguese control. In either event, however, they were elected in the area that they represented by people from the area. Thus this Congress was far more democratic than the first and came far closer to being a fully representative national body. The decisions made by it were in keeping with its composition; they signified a move towards a more democratic structure and a shift of political influence towards the party inside Mozambique.

The chief constitutional change made to bring the party structure up to date was in the composition and role of the Central Committee. Previously it had contained only the heads of departments and their assistants, and it had combined legislative, executive and judicial powers. The Congress expanded its membership to about 40, to include as well provincial secretaries, members elected by the provinces, members elected by the Congress, and representatives of mass organizations; and nearly all these new members were party leaders permanently resident in Mozambique. It also restricted the function of the new Central Committee to the legislative. To take over the role of the executive, a new organ was created, the Executive Committee, formed by the President, Vice-President, and secretaries of departments.

A political and military committee was created to deal with urgent problems that might arise between the ordinary meetings of the Central Committee. This consists of the President and Vice-President, the provincial secretaries, and the Secretaries of Defence, Security, Internal Organization and the Political Department.

The procedure for electing the party officers was clarified. The President and Vice-President are elected by the Congress upon proposal by the Central Committee, and their term of office lasts until the next Congress is called. The Congress should take place every four years.

Regional government was discussed and systematized. It was confirmed that each province has a provincial council and a provincial committee.

Economic organization

Production is of extreme and immediate importance, since it is necessary for the survival of the population, of the army and of any civilian services. In this context, food is obviously the first need.

With the overthrow of the colonial system, the companies which had imposed the production of cash crops either through plantations or the system of forced cultivation, withdrew. The people were free to organize agriculture as they wished and to concentrate on their own needs. As a result, after the war liberated a region, there was a return to the production of such basic food crops as maize, cassava, millet, beans, and groundnuts. But the war imposed additional demands on food producers. Although the military grow their own food wherever possible, there are inevitably large sections of the army which cannot be self-sufficient; also, to avoid reprisals from the Portuguese, it has been necessary in many areas to evacuate peasants and install them in new villages, where they need to be supplied with food until the first harvest from their new fields; in some areas a part of the crops is regularly destroyed by Portuguese action. Merely to satisfy food requirements over the liberated areas, therefore, it is necessary to produce a surplus.

The people are constantly encouraged to clear more land for cultivation and to grow more food, and this campaign has been so successful that, despite the hazards and upheavals of the war, more land is actually under cultivation today than there was during the colonial administration. Even after the first year of war, more food was being produced than before. Now in some areas, as at Ngazela, 80 per cent of the land cultivated had not previously been productive.

The greatest impetus to production has clearly come from the abolition of the companies, and from the fact that the people now themselves profit from their work. Two other factors are also important. One is the work of the party in advising, encouraging, and explaining the needs of the struggle, and in providing essential pieces of equipment like hoes and pangas. The other, linked with this, is the development of new methods of organization, principally the cooperative. In areas where there had been a cooperative movement before the struggle, the organization reappeared rapidly and spontaneously after the colonial forces had been expelled. In other areas, the idea has been introduced, and party members have had to help the people get them started. Instruction in book-keeping has been a particularly important aspect. Between the liberated areas, there are considerable differences in the stage of development that the cooperative system has reached. In some, all production may be organized collectively; in others, the people work *shambas* individually, to supply their own family needs, but the village as a whole works other *shambas* cooperatively, to produce a surplus for the army or other groups unable to produce. In some areas the people have not formed cooperatives at all, mainly because they lack the necessary knowledge of how to organize them and keep the accounts, and in such cases a surplus is produced by a system whereby many of the villagers individually cultivate an extra *shamba* to produce food for collective needs.

FRELIMO is at present studying various ways of developing agriculture, to improve yields, promote variety and develop the production of crops for export. The high plateau of Niassa is ideally suited for market gardening, and we are hoping to introduce there many types of fruit and vegetable which will improve the diet of the population and eventually provide a source of income for them.

Apart from the surplus which must be grown to satisfy our own needs, a further surplus must be produced for export, to provide us with the means of importing essentials such as cloth which we cannot for a long time hope to produce ourselves on any significant scale. We have already been able to export a few items in 1966:

	Tons
Cashew nuts	500
Sesame seed	100
Groundnuts	100
Castor oil seed	10

We are trying to expand the production of oil seed for export and at the moment some of the cooperatives are experimenting with the reintroduction of cotton as a cash crop. Tobacco is grown fairly extensively in some of the liberated areas; but up to now we have lacked the technical knowledge to cure the leaf properly, and it has been used only in a rough form for home consumption. We have now, however, sent some people abroad to train in this field, and we hope shortly to add tobacco to our exports. Over the last two years we have also been researching into the various types of rubber which grow in Northern Mozambique, with a view to making this into another source of income.

The other side to this attempt at producing goods for export is the struggle to reduce imports. Except where the war has badly disrupted production, the population is, or can be made, self-sufficient in foodstuffs; but clothes, agricultural implements, salt, soap, and other such everyday products must all be supplied. At present, we are importing these items in carefully limited quantities, for distribution through trading cooperatives, formed to take over the work of the trade network which virtually collapsed when the Portuguese left the area. Because of our inadequate resources, however, and the problems of transport, it is not possible to maintain adequate supplies in this way, and we are researching into methods of producing such goods inside the country. Salt is already being extracted in the north-east. Soap could be manufactured from oil seed if we could obtain the necessary plant and have some of our people trained in the process. Traditional crafts are being encouraged to supply the immediate need for household and simple agricultural implements.

These crafts have also become another source of exports. The Makonde people in particular are famous for their woodcarving and sculpture. Under the influence of the Portuguese, the tradition had been somewhat bastardized, both through the pressure of missionaries on artists to produce imitations of European religious works and through traders demanding 'assembly line' production of curios for the tourist market. In 1967, when FRELIMO first organized the export of several hundred woodcarvings from inside Mozambique, the majority were of this stereotyped nature; but there were also several original pieces of very considerable artistic merit. We tried immediately to encourage the artists who had produced them and explain to others that work of that type, although slower, was far more valuable than the production of mere curios. We also explored ways of selling such works to genuine collectors in Europe and the United States, and are trying to organize the production and sale of these pieces so that the producers themselves may benefit fairly.

Education

When FRELIMO was first formed, we gave top priority jointly to two programmes: the military and the educational. We have always attached such great importance to education because, in the first place, it is essential for the development of our struggle, since the involvement and support of the population increase as their understanding of the situation grows; in the second place, a future independent Mozambique will be in very grave need of educated citizens to lead the way in development.

The Portuguese system of education has been hopelessly inadequate, not only because it has involved so very few Africans, but also because the instruction given to those few was so unsuited to the needs of Mozambique. We have had to start working from scratch, not only in providing the structure but in working out the content.

Schooling in most African countries uses a system designed to meet the needs of late nineteenth-century Europe. It is now recognized even in Europe that this system is out of date and that much of it is irrelevant. In Africa, it never did and certainly does not now answer the real needs of the population. All colonial education was designed essentially to produce a small Europeanized élite who would either serve or take over from the colonial government, to preserve its values. Every effort was made to cut these people off from their origins, partly because most Europeans despised every aspect of African culture and partly because the élite would thus present less of a threat to European government. The colonial régimes completely ignored existing indigenous methods of education and acted as if there had been no education at all before the Europeans opened schools.

It is realized now, even outside Africa, that this was an extremely narrow conception of what education is. Theorists now generally divide education into two types, the formal and the informal, and all societies have always used both types in different degrees. Informal education consists in overt training by elders, in the emulation of older children by younger ones, in observation at ceremonies, in listening to stories, in watching and helping adults go about their daily tasks. This type of education includes the inculcation of moral values and proper conduct, by correcting infringements of the accepted code, by admonition, ridicule or punishment, and in the praise of admired behaviour.

In simple rural communities, this system of education is adequate in preparing the young adolescent to fit into the day-to-day life of his society. But as society grows large and simple means of production become inadequate, it is necessary to develop more formal systems of educating the young. In different parts of Africa, this situation developed several thousands of years ago. The earliest type of formal system is the so-called initiation school, common in so many African areas, with the 'secret societies' performing similar functions. Every secret society provides in its initiation rites a certain amount of social knowledge and instruction which enables the individual to cope with his immediate environment. The 'bush' schools of the Poro and Sande, for example, are highly developed institutions, where the initiate is trained under strict discipline for obedience to the rules of society and to the social regulations of the large community. He is put through a series of tough situations – including little sleep, hard labour, long walks and uncomfortable living quarters – which, like the European 'outward bound' schools, are intended to teach both moral qualities and practical skills. Training may include some traditional law and custom, illustrated by mock courts and trials; and often arts, crafts, agricultural or hunting techniques. Singing and dancing in groups usually plays an important part in the life of these initiation schools.

The great virtues of this precolonial African education were that it was directly geared to the needs of the society, that it was totally integrated, and that it extended to everyone equally. There were cases of special initiation courses for particular groups, like seers, witch-doctors, craftsmen; but these existed side by side with a universal system, of which they were only a specialized part.

The societies in which such systems evolved, however, were confined to small areas and based on a fairly simple economy. As new complexities were introduced they became inadequate; for new types of knowledge, new skills were needed. The schools of missionaries and colonial governments, for all their faults, offered Africans the opportunity of learning some of the skills needed to cope with the new conditions. In return, however, the Africans were forced to sacrifice their social values and customs, to reject their past. This caused extreme tension both in the individual and in the society.

If, to a large extent, this split was simply accepted or else the European culture altogether rejected, there were some Africans who realized that European skills were not inseparable from European values. An early attempt to act on this realization was the establishment of the Kikuyu Independent schools in Kenya, after the mission schools refused to accept circumcised girls. But these new schools did no more than try to combine the European curricula with traditional Kikuyu society.

What is needed is more than a straight combination. A new factor is involved: the development of the independent national state. For neither the traditional nor the colonial system of education is designed to fit the needs of this new entity. A new departure is required. But a departure must begin somewhere. We can learn from other cultures, including the European, but we cannot graft them directly on to our own. It is for this reason that a certain understanding of our own cultures and our own past is essential. Much of our traditional education is obsolete; but some aspects – the art and some of the moral values, for instance – can help form a basis for the new society we are trying to build. As Jahn put it: 'Only where man feels himself to be heir and successor to the past has he the strength for a new beginning.'

The immediate context within which we are working is that of the national liberation struggle and the accompanying social revolution. It is this which must mould the new aspects of the educational service we are developing. As society is changing with the struggle, so we must be prepared for education to change. In the short run, though, there are urgent practical purposes which must be served: we need educated cadres at all levels and in all disciplines; we need to raise the abysmally low educational level of the general population, to fight illiteracy and ignorance. We must start working on this now with what we have available, and develop our theory and system as we work.

As soon as the war had liberated some areas, small primary schools were started with very rudimentary equipment. By 1966 there were 100 of these schools in Cabo Delgado alone, catering for about 10,000 children and with a teacher ratio varying from 250:1 to 25:1. Towards the end of 1967, ten teachers started work setting up schools in Niassa, and by the end of the year 2,000 children were receiving education there. Because of the tremendous shortage of trained personnel many of the teachers themselves have studied no further than primary school, and the education given in these schools is thus necessarily of a rather rudimentary nature. But it is at least geared to the needs of the children in the context of their own culture and the national struggle. They learn Portuguese, since this is our common language, but also the history and geography of Mozambique. Reading, writing, arithmetic and civics are the main subjects taught. In civics they learn about our country and its background, about the war and the aims of FRELIMO, and something about the rest of Africa and the world. The need to be self-sufficient and at the same time to work with other people for a common good is learnt as much through practical work as in the formal classes. As far as possible the schools cultivate their own fields, and make their own clothes and equipment, while to help overcome the lack of teachers, more advanced children may be asked to help the less advanced, join in adult literacy campaigns, or undertake other tasks in areas where their schooling qualifies them.

The primary school programme is only part of the work done by the Department of Education. As well as facing the problem of mass illiteracy, we suffer from an almost total lack of trained people in almost every field. The Department of Education has to try and remedy this by arranging higher education and various specialized courses for selected young people who have already had some basic schooling. Some of this is achieved through the Mozambique Institute which still functions in Dar es Salaam, although the scope and nature of its work have changed considerably since it was first founded in 1963. Established originally as a tutorial centre, which rapidly developed into a secondary school for Mozambican refugees, the Institute was at first financed by a Ford Foundation grant; but as this was withdrawn the following year, it had to raise its funds from other sources and is now supported from a variety of countries and organizations, with the largest sums at present coming from Scandinavia.

Early on, the Institute became financially responsible for primary schools as well, set up to provide education at this level for Mozambican refugees in Tanzania. It was therefore natural that, when the war started, the Institute should be called on to find funds for the new primary schools in Mozambique and for other new programmes made necessary by the war and the creation of liberated areas. These last included a number of new courses organized by FRELIMO in association with the Institute and run with the help of some Institute staff. The first was a course for nurses, preparing them to take part in the new medical programme for Mozambique. This was followed by the establishment of a political and administrative course for those working in local government in the newly liberated areas. In 1968 a course for primary school teachers was added.

This is as far as FRELIMO's own educational services have been able to go up to now; but, in addition, FRELIMO and the Institute cooperate in organizing scholarships abroad for Mozambicans so that they can take academic and technical courses at a more advanced level. It has been our firm policy since the beginning, however, that all education arranged by FRELIMO – whether it takes place inside Mozambique, in neighbouring Tanzania, in a Mozambican community, or abroad in a foreign college or institute – must be an integral part of the national struggle; all students must regard their training as a means of fitting them to work in Mozambique, and they must be ready to return at any time that they should be called upon to do so. There have been considerable problems with students who pretend not

179

to understand, or who refuse to accept this policy. This is partly due to the fact that the educational programme began before the armed struggle, and some of the students now studying abroad or in the secondary school have no experience of the war or of life in the liberated areas, so that it appears either frightening or unreal to them. Several students sent abroad in 1963 have refused to return at the end of their courses, and a number of students from the secondary school objected violently against going back to work in Mozambique, demanding that they should be sent to continue higher studies immediately. These difficulties have caused us to lose a number of educated people who could have given useful service. But it has also led to an even firmer and more realistic policy on education; to greater efforts at integrating studies with the struggle and at preventing in the future the formation of groups who demand special privileges at the expense of the general population. Several practical changes are planned for the future. As far as possible, young people will be selected for further studies outside Mozambique only after they have spent some time working either in the army or in the civilian services. Secondly, more emphasis will be placed on short courses in specific skills, such as the nurses and administrators' courses in Tanzania or short technical courses abroad. Thirdly, all students will be required to return for a term of service after their schooling is finished. More effort will be made to keep in touch with those engaged abroad on long courses, and to encourage them in such work for the struggle as they are able to do there by spreading information and interesting people in Mozambique. Most important of all, an even greater effort will be made to improve facilities inside Mozambique, so that more people can receive their education on the spot.

Health

Like most of the countries of Africa, Mozambique has very serious public health problems: tropical diseases like malaria, bilharzia, sleeping sickness and yaws are endemic, and there are periodic epidemics of smallpox, typhoid, yellow fever and other highly infectious diseases. The Portuguese health services did very little to improve this situation. Outside the towns there were practically no health centres; vaccination campaigns were inadequate and rarely even attempted in the more isolated rural areas; nearly all the hospitals and qualified doctors were located in the few major towns, to treat paying patients and so in effect only the European population and a few others. An indication of the Portuguese achievement is that Mozambique has one of the highest rates of infant mortality in Africa.

The immediate effect of the war was to make the situation even worse. Such health centres as the Portuguese had set up in the north were immediately withdrawn; the rapid population shifts and the creation of large numbers of refugees made the people a prey to epidemics, while the fighting and Portuguese air raids added war casualties to the many already in need of medical attention.

FRELIMO had to organize its own health service, starting pretty well from scratch. The problems were, and still are, enormous. There was neither the money nor the trained personnel. As a result of the poor education provided by the Portuguese, there is not a single African qualified doctor in the whole of Mozambique, and there are few medical aides and nurses. Thus the medical programme had to tackle two tasks at once; it had immediately to organize some sort of medical relief inside Mozambique with what few resources could be found, and at the same time arrange rapidly to train more medical staff.

An administrative structure was devised whereby the liberated areas are divided into medical regions and districts. In each, there are a number of health centres, varying from simple first aid posts to small clinics where minor surgery and ligatures can be done. These centres are linked with one another, so that when necessary a case can be transferred from a smaller unit to a larger and better equipped one. Drugs and equipment are still in desperately short supply, and some of the first aid posts periodically run out of even basic antiseptic and bandages. All the same, the bulk of the population is now better served than it ever was under the Portuguese, when there was no organized free medical service.

Another field where FRELIMO has already achieved more than the Portuguese is that of preventive medicine. From the beginning this was considered a high priority, and great efforts were made to obtain vaccines. By 1967 a number of localized campaigns against typhoid, tetanus and tuberculosis had been carried out, and a mass campaign against smallpox was under way in which, by September 1967, 100,000 people had been vaccinated. The main problem has been, and still is, that of getting enough vaccine. Administratively, the health service has the great advantage of working with the party structure, through which such campaigns and their purpose can be explained to the whole population. Given adequate supplies of vaccine, it would, for this reason, be possible to vaccinate the whole population in a relatively short space of time.

Another aspect of preventive medicine is health education, and in this, also, the service benefits from close integration with the party, the army, and the educational service. Health education is taught in schools and in the army, with teachers and militants helping to spread a basic knowledge of hygiene among the whole population.

As well as working to improve conditions in the present, the medical service has been studying the health problems of the people and collecting its own medical statistics (since those gathered by the Portuguese have been found very inaccurate) so as to help in planning for the future.

Personnel as well as equipment is still, and will continue to be, a great problem. The nurses' course, run in association with the Mozambique Institute, has graduated two classes, and a number of students are abroad studying medicine. Two white Mozambican doctors working with FRELIMO took a very important part in the planning of the health service and the training programmes, but there is still not one qualified doctor in the liberated areas of Mozambique. In this, as in every other field, the shortage of people with the basic qualifications to start specialized courses impedes progress tremendously, and in this respect the future of the medical programme will depend on the success of the work done in education. At least now there exists a structure and a programme which will ensure a gradual improvement in the situation, and which can deploy such qualified people as become available.

Social and cultural development

Already as a result of the struggle, profound changes have occurred in the life of the people in the liberated and semi-liberated areas. These changes comprise much more than the removal of the colonial structure and its influence; forms of government, of social and economic organization, have been introduced which are essentially new, owing their origin only marginally to African traditional life and not at all to the colonial system.

In culture, perhaps, the traditional elements are strongest, since in this field they are not inconsistent with the growth of the nation. The Portuguese government attempted to clamp down not only on the political life of the African but also on all other traditional aspects, his art, his language, his customs. This did not mean that the traditional way of life disappeared; it survived as a somewhat subdued 'underground' culture, frowned upon and openly despised by the authorities. With the expulsion of the Portuguese, there has been a natural resurgence, which in some directions has been encouraged by the revolution; in the schools and in the military camps, traditional songs and dances are practised. In the producers' cooperatives, the arts and crafts are developed. Yet even within this traditional framework, there are a number of new developments. For instance, in the camps, the young people are not only practising the songs and dances of their own tribe, but learning those of others, while in the fields of production new ideas and techniques are being introduced both from different areas of Mozambique and from outside. Then, the struggle itself is making its mark in the form of new themes for songs and new themes in art. For example the FRELIMO guerrilla has appeared among the many figures which the Makonde sculptors carve.

Apart from encouraging traditional African arts, FRELIMO has also produced a flow of ideas from a variety of other cultures. The Portuguese, as far as they brought new ideas to Africa, brought only those of their own country. Now the source is much wider: in the camps militants may learn the songs of the Russian revolution, read magazines from Cuba, see pictures of life in Vietnam. At the Mozambique Institute and at camps where it is possible, documentary films are shown from all over the world. In the course of their education and training, student militants are sent to a wide variety of countries, from the United States to the People's Republic of China, and to some extent spread their knowledge of these countries among their companions when they return. At the moment, in the conditions of war, with the lack of resources and facilities and the lack of education, these developments have had little effect beyond the schools and the army; but in those sectors already, people know something more about the rest of the world than they did before the struggle.

Before the struggle, writing and reading were aspects of life virtually unknown to the population outside the major towns. Neither literacy campaigns, nor the production and supply of literature, have developed far enough to have changed this significantly as yet. The popular attitude has begun to change, however. The schools and work in adult literacy have shown that the written word is something that can and will belong to the world of ordinary people, to the country as well as the towns, and there is now a great desire to learn. Among the militants, this desire is fast being satisfied. Many still cannot read, write or cope with Portuguese; but some can, and of these not a few are using their ability creatively as well as for practical purposes. There is a magazine produced by the militants for the militants called *25 de setembro*, to which everyone is free to contribute. In it, poems, stories and political analyses are published; the opportunity given to a wide range of people to have their work printed and discussed, stimulates and develops their abilities.

Such activities have also given a new significance to the work of the more sophisticated writers. When Craveirinha and Noémia de Sousa were writing their eloquent denunciations of Portuguese colonialism, they were not read by the people they were writing for and about. Now the work of a good poet in FRELIMO will be read in the camps by the militants, by people drawn from the exploited masses who in the past were simply the subjects of poems by poets they had never heard of. Now those who can read, read aloud for those who cannot, and a wealth of literature is in reach of all those who have a minimum grasp of Portuguese. The gap between the intellectual and the rest of the population is closing. And this in turn has brought a new dimension to political poetry, which has lost its tone of lament and gained a new revolutionary fire, as in the poems of Marcelino dos Santos, Jorge Rebelo, Armando Guebuza, Sérgio Vieira. The essence of this new dimension is summed up in these extracts from Jorge Rebelo's 'Poem', in which he calls on a comrade to speak of 'dreams of revolt' and of 'these dreams [which] become war', for then he will

. . . forge simple words
that even the children can understand
words which will enter every house
like the wind
and fall, like red hot embers
on our people's souls.

For, as the poet ends,

In our land
bullets are beginning to flower.

The culture of the revolution is growing only slowly and taking its place alongside traditional culture; but the social changes which are its base are proceeding much more rapidly. With the growth of entirely new political and economic structures, lives and outlooks have changed fundamentally.

The position of the woman is one of the most striking aspects of this. In African society, as in Portuguese, the woman has held a more or less subject position. The extent and nature of subjection has varied very much from region to region: in some instances, as René Dumont points out in his discussion of present-day African problems, *False Start in Africa*,* she has suffered a type of economic exploitation, having to bear the brunt of the labour necessary to support the whole society; in others, she has suffered from social restrictions and been denied a place of any influence

* Deutsch, 1966.

in the family or in the larger community. Now the drive to produce more is forcing everyone to take a fair share of the daily work, and the part that women are playing in the Mozambique liberation army and the party is changing attitudes towards them, bringing men to respect them and giving them a new voice in the running of affairs. Josina Abiathar Muthemba, a woman militant, describes this:

Before the struggle, even in our society women had an inferior position. Today in FRELIMO the Mozambican woman has a voice and an important role to play; she can express her opinions; she is free to say what she likes. She has the same rights and duties as any militant, because she is Mozambican, because in our party there is no discrimination based on sex. (F.I.)

This development has in no way been forced on women from above. It is very largely due to their own action now that it is continuing. For example, when I addressed a meeting in Mozambique early in 1968, and the people began asking questions, a woman in one of the women's units got up and complained that women were not being trained as officers, so that all the officers were men. Why was this, she demanded to know. The reason was that nobody had thought of making women officers. As a result of her criticism, however, a decision was taken that in the future women would be able to become officers when they had suitable qualifications and experience.

This example illustrates the general pattern of social change in other spheres as well. The struggle is the initial impetus, and while the leadership is often called upon to provide the means to promote new developments, the movement comes very much from the people. At that same meeting, there was another instance of this. We were discussing production, and the villagers described what they were doing to increase it. They had not organized a cooperative but were cultivating additional individual *shambas* to produce a surplus. They told us that they had wanted to organize themselves cooperatively, but they were unable to do so because no one knew anything about book-keeping; they asked the party leaders to provide them with someone who could teach them what they needed to know, so that they could take this step themselves.

The change in the position of women is also indicative of the more general transformation in attitudes. The customs, beliefs and superstitions which used to sanction various kinds of inequality and exploitation are gradually being shed together with the practices they encouraged. The first condition for this has been the destruction of colonial government, the main perpetrator of inequality and exploitation, and this has been achieved in a fifth of the country. In these areas, the people will testify to the improvements which have taken place, despite the hardships imposed by the war. This is how three ordinary militants, who have been fighting over wide areas of the country, put it:

Gabriel Maurício Nantimbo: Now there is the war. If I compare the present with the past, I see that in my region the people have a better life. There are difficulties but it's different. When the people produce crops now, they eat better; the companies don't come to rob them; there is no forced labour; our people are free; we can say that the war is liberating the people.

Joaquim Maquival: The war has changed the people's situation. Where the war has already broken out, the people are no longer beaten, there are no longer taxes which exploit the people, the people are not humiliated. There are hardships but this is the price of victory.

Rita Mulumbua (woman): The revolution is transforming our life. Before I was ignorant, while now I speak in front of everyone at meetings. We are united. We discuss our problems among ourselves and that reinforces our unity.

The Second Congress

The Second Congress of FRELIMO, held in Niassa province in July 1968, was clear evidence of the various changes already described; the decisions made at it are the guarantee that these changes will continue.

The fact that the Congress could be held at all was proof of the success achieved by the military programme. For the event took months to prepare, it was announced publicly in advance, it involved the presence in one place of the whole party executive and military leadership, and yet it passed with no interference from the Portuguese, in territory which the Portuguese still claim to control.

The accomplishments of our political organization were shown by the presence of delegates from all over Mozambique, even from the far south. Here for the first time in our history Mozambicans from all over the country were gathered, to discuss together the problems of the whole nation and take decisions which will affect its future. Delegates were from different tribes and different religious groups, and there were women participating as well as men. This in itself is an indication of the distance we have come in the last four years.

Although we were holding the Congress inside Mozambique, we were even able to invite a number of foreign observers. There were two representatives of the Afro-Asian Solidarity Organization, a representative of the People's Movement for the Liberation of Angola, a representative of the African National Congress of South Africa, and a representative from ZAPU (the Zimbabwe African Peoples' Union).

Apart from electing officials and making the constitutional changes described earlier, the Congress discussed every aspect of the struggle, clarified questions of policy and made numerous detailed decisions. The delegates from each region and the heads of departments presented reports describing their work over the last few years and outlining plans for the future. These then became the basis for an open discussion on each topic, in which every delegate was able to ask questions and make criticisms and suggestions. A series of resolutions were then drafted and put to the Congress. These give a clear outline of our policy and aims for the next four years. Essentially these resolutions re-affirm the need for an armed struggle and the importance of simultaneously developing those areas which, as a result of the armed struggle, come under our control. They also indicate a new drive to increase the efficiency of organization and administration by setting down precise patterns for administrative structure and clarifying the functions of different bodies. But the ground covered was so wide that an adequate picture can only be gained from citing some of the resolutions themselves:

Resolutions on the armed struggle

1. The Portuguese government is a colonialist, fascist government that still maintains the myth that Mozambique is a Portuguese Province, and, consequently, 'part and parcel of Portugal'. It still does not recognize the right of the Mozambican people to their national independence.

Nationalist demonstrations are violently repressed with massacres, jailings, tortures, assassinations.

Under these conditions, and in order to face all forms of colonialist oppression and repression, the Mozambican people have decided to follow resolutely the way of armed struggle, by fighting a decisive war of independence or death.

2. The Portuguese colonialists have dominated and exploited the Mozambican people for a very long time. Today, they still have the control of the means of production in those regions of Mozambique where they exert their domination.

Their military force is a powerful one. Besides the army, they have an air force and navy. Despite the rapid growth of our military power, the Portuguese colonialist army is even stronger. On the other hand, we still have great material needs. We need weapons, medicines, means of transport, etc., which, at this phase of our struggle, we have to get from abroad. We also need technicians. So that, with respect to the supply of material and training of technicians, we shall continue for some time to depend on external aid.

Furthermore, the geographical and political situation of our country, as well as the political situation of the neighbouring countries – Swaziland, South Africa, Rhodesia, Malawi – makes it difficult to extend the war further to the South. To carry war material into Zambézia, Moçambique, Manica e Sofala, Inhambane, Gaza and Lourenço Marques Provinces, we have to overcome many difficulties.

All these factors put together build the existing imbalance of forces between us and the enemy. Though politically stronger, we are still militarily weak. In order to get our victory, we have no other way out but to change the direction of this imbalance; we will do it, but for that a great effort is required from us. Our war will therefore be a hard and long one.

3. Our struggle is a people's struggle. It requires the total participation of all the masses of the people. For this reason it is necessary to intensify the mobilization and the organization of the masses in the liberated zones, as well as in the regions where the armed struggle has not yet started.

The direct participation of all in the armed struggle is, therefore, one of the main objectives of the people's mobilization effort.

In the present phase of our struggle, our main armed forces are made up of the regular guerrilla forces, but people's militias do also play a very important role. People's militias are part and parcel of the population. They are supplementary to the guerrilla forces and they are fixed in the territory in which they work. All the people – old, young, women and men – who are not part of the guerrillas, must be part of the militias.

People's militias should at the same time satisfy the needs of production, vigilance and defence. In the liberated and semi-liberated zones, people's militias do in particular the following work:

(1) transport of material and the sick;
(2) reconnaissance and patrol of the zones in which they work against the infiltration of enemy troops and agents;
(3) fighting, when the enemy invades the region.
   People's militias do take part in heavy fighting, when that is called for.

The organization of people's militias is an important form of integrating the masses into the armed struggle. In this way, at every place, sufficient and militarily prepared forces are created. People's militias are therefore reserve forces.

4. In order to realize more completely and efficiently the participation of the Mozambican women in the struggle, a women's detachment has been created whose main functions are:

(1) mobilization and organization of the masses;
(2) recruitment of young people of both sexes to be integrated into the armed struggle;
(3) production;
(4) transport of material;
(5) military protection for the populations.

5. The phenomenon of desertion is not a specific characteristic of the struggle for liberation of Mozambique. There are desertions in most countries, even in the absence of war.

In the movement for National Liberation of Mozambique, desertions have many causes.

Many comrades are engaged in the struggle because they really have a nationalist, political conscience. But there are some whose national feeling is very weak. There are others who, after committing transgressions, fear punishment by the Portuguese authorities. Then, to escape from punishment, they engage themselves in the nationalist movement. Persons with such a behaviour often fail: they are unable to withstand the difficult guerrilla's life, and they can hardly acquire nationalist, political conscience. So they desert. And once out of the movement, they give themselves to inventing excuses to justify themselves. Some spread every kind of rumour in order to discredit the leaders, divorce them from the masses, and disintegrate the struggle. Others give themselves up to the Portuguese. Desertions are grave crimes. Deserters are enemies of the Mozambican people.

6. Prisoners of war have a political importance for us. We should treat them well. Through them, we can obtain information on the enemy. We should re-educate them as much as possible, and, according to our interests, eventually let them free.

We may also use prisoners as hostages to be exchanged for our comrades who may be in the Portuguese colonial prisons. In this way, we would be showing to the world that we are fighting against Portuguese colonialism and not against the Portuguese people; we would be breaking the fighting morale of the enemy's army, and encouraging its soldiers' desertions.

The Second Congress decides, therefore, that FRELIMO should continue to apply the policy of clemency with regard to captured enemy soldiers.

7. Our war is essentially a political war, and its direction is defined by the party. The people's army is part and parcel of the party, and its strategic plans are made by the top leadership of the party.

In order to conduct correctly the struggle, all the leaders should be involved in the armed struggle. Only in this way, following the struggle step by step, the leaders can be able to solve all the complex problems arising daily. The people's army performs its task in accordance with the policy defined by FRELIMO.

Resolutions on administration of the liberated zones

1. The administration of the liberated zones aims at establishing the people's power. Only through an adequate administration will it be possible to consolidate the defence of the liberated zones, to promote its growth and the economic and social progress of the people, and thus to lay the basis for a victorious development of the revolutionary, armed struggle for national liberation.

The direction of the administration in the liberated zones will be undertaken by committees at the several organic levels of FRELIMO, Provincial, District, Local, etc., – as stated in the general regulations.

People's management committees, elected by the people themselves shall be created, whenever possible, to supervise general tasks.

The Provincial Committee, the District Committee or the Local Committee, each at its level, shall direct the establishment of these people's management committees, and shall render them, whenever needed and as much as possible, the necessary technical assistance.

2. The Second Congress maintains that only when the provincial structures are functioning conveniently, will it be possible to administer correctly the liberated zones. For this reason the Second Congress rules that:

   (1) Clear guidance shall be given to the various provincial organs, so that they may realize completely their functions.

   (2) Adequate control system for the provincial organs shall be organized.

   (3) Leaders of FRELIMO shall make frequent visits to the provinces.

   (4) The various positions in each of the provincial organs shall be conveniently and effectively filled.

   (5) Necessary sections shall be established which shall function under the provincial administration.

   (6) Training of technical cadres needed by the provinces shall be accelerated.

3. Furthermore, the Second Congress rules that:

   (1) Provincial budgets shall essentially depend on the production of the province.

   (2) All necessary efforts shall be made so that Mozambicans who have sought refuge abroad may return to Mozambique.

   (3) Judicial committees shall be created which shall look over the execution of the laws.

Resolutions on national reconstruction

1. The Second Congress notes that the building of a new life in the liberated zones is a requirement of the struggle for national liberation. The liberated zones shall constitute the material basis for growth of our revolutionary armed struggle for national liberation. In that sense, the growth of production assumes special importance.

It is necessary for us to produce progressively the material goods we need for the growth of our armed struggle. We should promote the development of agriculture, industry, cottage industries, always directing our activities towards the meeting of the interests of our people's revolution.

Hand in hand with production, we shall develop commerce, both internal and external. We should also promote the development of education and health services. At the same time, we should promote our national culture by developing the positive values of our regional customs now enriched by our effort to create a new reality: a united and free Mozambique.

All these aspects of our efforts for national reconstruction are closely connected, and for efficiency of work, it is imperative that all sectors of our activity be perfectly coordinated, without which, all our efforts will be useless.

To carry on our work, we have to overcome various difficulties and solve many problems, some very pressing ones, such as population dispersion into small settlements separated by large distances, the lack of means of communication, the scarcity of cadres. In order to face these problems, measures shall be taken with a view to:

(1) promoting, whenever possible, the resettlement of the population;

(2) encouraging Mozambican refugees in neighbouring countries to return to Mozambique in order to take part in national reconstruction tasks;

(3) intensifying the training of cadres necessary for the execution of the various tasks dictated by the Revolution.

Whenever deemed necessary and indispensable, foreign technicians shall be recruited, who accept to follow the political line and the programme of FRELIMO.

2. More specifically, the Second Congress of FRELIMO rules that:

On production and commerce

(1) Agricultural production shall be developed, such that we may get all we need for food as well as the raw materials for production of soap, fabrics, etc.

(2) Technical and scientific level of production shall be promoted.

(3) Defence of agriculture fields shall be more and more consolidated.

(4) Organization of agricultural, commercial, and industrial cooperatives shall be developed.

On education

(1) Development of primary schools shall be accelerated.

(2) Teacher training programme for primary schools shall be

developed in order to raise rapidly its numbers and its technical level.

(3) Intensive literacy campaigns among the masses of the people, men, women, old and young people shall be promoted.

(4) Special courses for raising rapidly the level of knowledge of the militants shall be organized.

(5) Young Mozambican women shall be encouraged to complete at least primary school education.

(6) Production centres shall be created at every school place for self-maintenance.

(7) A system shall be established which shall make it possible for the students to interrupt temporarily their studies in order to participate in teaching and literacy campaigns.

(8) It shall be the duty of all Mozambican students to take part, whenever it may be deemed necessary, in the various tasks of the struggle for national liberation.

(9) Development of schools of political training shall be promoted.

On health

(1) Intensive campaigns shall be promoted for obtaining medicines and medical supplies, throughout the world.

(2) Establishment of medical centres shall be promoted in the regions that will be successively liberated.

(3) Organization of transport of medicines and medical supplies shall be organized for the various regions.

Resolutions on social affairs

The growth of the Mozambican Revolution requires that particular attention be given to the social conditions of the masses.

A correct direction that will promote the satisfaction of the social needs of the masses will also raise their revolutionary spirit, and will at the same time avoid that the difficulties, normal in a war situation, may turn into serious obstacles to the progress of the war for national liberation.

So, therefore, the Second Congress rules that:

(1) Necessary measures shall be taken to improve the material conditions of the masses in the war zones, particularly with respect to satisfaction of primary needs, such as salt, soap, clothing.

(2) Institutions for social assistance, as well as for study and suggestion of solutions to problems on social relationships, particularly those concerning marriage, shall be created at the provincial level.

(3) Particular attention shall be given to the wives of the militants, seeing to it that whenever possible, they are fixed in the provinces where their husbands are fighting, and encouraging those outside the country to return home.

(4) Whenever possible, pregnant women and those with little babies shall be settled in zones of greater stability.

(5) FRELIMO, in cooperation with LIFEMO,* shall establish the ways in which the latter shall take care of the orphan children; the same care shall be given to the children of unmarried women, in order to give a chance to the latter to contribute to the struggle.

(6) Conditions for assistance and rehabilitation of the war disabled shall be created.

Resolutions on foreign policy

1. The Mozambican people are engaged in an armed struggle against Portuguese colonialism and imperialism for their national independence and for the establishment of a social, democratic order in Mozambique.

This struggle is part of the world's movement for the emancipation of the peoples, which aims at the total liquidation of colonialism and imperialism, and at the construction of a new society free from exploitation of man by man.

For this reason, FRELIMO has created and developed solidarity and friendly relations with peoples, organizations and governments fighting for the realization of these objectives. FRELIMO has established relations with nationalist organizations of the Portuguese colonies, and with nationalist organizations of other African countries still under foreign domination.

FRELIMO has relations with progressive organizations of Asian-African and Latin American countries. FRELIMO has relations with all socialist countries, and with progressive countries of the West. FRELIMO is a member of the following international organizations:

(1) CONCP – Conference of Nationalist Organizations of the Portuguese colonies;

* The women's organization of FRELIMO.

    (2) OAU – Organization of African Unity;

    (3) OSPAA – Afro-Asian Peoples' Solidarity Organization;

    (4) OSPAAAL – Afro-Asian Latin American Peoples' Solidarity Organization;

    (5) WCP – World Council of Peace.

The Second Congress declares that FRELIMO and the Mozambican people shall continue to develop and consolidate their alliances and to give their maximum contribution to the world people's movement against colonialism and imperialism for economic, political, social and cultural emancipation of peoples and for the construction of a new society free from exploitation of man by man.

2. The struggle in which the Mozambican people, under the leadership of FRELIMO, are engaged in against Portuguese colonialism and imperialism, enjoys the world's sympathy and support.

The Second Congress highly appreciates the aid given by the peoples, organizations and governments of African countries to the liberation struggle of the Mozambican people, in particular through the African Liberation Committee.

The Second Congress points out in particular the aid given by TANU, the people and government of Tanzania, under the leadership of President Mwalimu Julius Nyerere, to the anti-colonialist, national liberation struggle of the Mozambican people, directed by FRELIMO.

Among the African countries, the Second Congress stresses also the high contribution given the Mozambican people's struggle by Algeria, the United Arab Republic and Zambia, either through the OAU or bilaterally.

The Second Congress highly appreciates and hails the aid given the Mozambican people by socialist countries of Europe and Asia, which aid has been a great contribution for the success of the Mozambican Revolution.

The Second Congress appreciates the aid given to the Mozambican people's struggle by the revolutionary people and government of Cuba.

9 International Relations

We are in Africa because it is our right, our duty and our interest. But we are in Africa because that is also the general interest of the free world.

Alberto Franco Noguira, Portuguese Foreign Minister

In Africa the dividing line between the white dominated South and the independent states to the north is hardening. In South Africa the policy of apartheid is being ruthlessly pursued, with the operations of the police state expanding to enforce it. The long period of passive resistance there has virtually come to an end, killed by the increasing violence of repression. The South African state has also, in defiance of the United Nations, tightened its grip on South West Africa. In Rhodesia, the white settler rebellion has brought the territory firmly into the South African sphere of influence and put an end to hopes of democratic progress towards majority rule. Portuguese authority which has for a long time appeared somewhat isolated, considered as backward and inefficient by the other white powers, has now established close political, military and economic links with the other minority governments of Southern Africa.

Opposition movements have recently been undergoing important transformation. Peaceful and constitutional methods of agitation are now officially denied them, and as a result they are turning to underground activity and the techniques of armed revolution.

These movements naturally look towards independent Africa as their ally in the struggle. If assistance is given, though, this courts reprisals from the white governments. Zambia, in particular, is critically placed, bordering as she does on Mozambique, Angola and Rhodesia; she has already suffered a number of air attacks by Portuguese forces on border villages, and has been openly threatened on several occasions by the Rhodesian and South African authorities.

A state of overall confrontation is developing which cannot be contained within Africa. As hostilities escalate, sudden and important political changes become possible; the major powers are drawn in, and the struggle becomes a world issue.

As a number of journalists and politicians have pointed out, the return of the Cape route to the foreground with the closing of the Suez Canal has highlighted the international significance of Southern Africa, but this is only one facet of the situation. Europe had economic interests in Africa even before the days of political expansion, and during the colonial period these grew to considerable proportions. The movement for independence has only marginally affected the relationship. France and Britain still have extensive investments in their former colonies, and in some instances are busily increasing them. Not seldom, independence has made it easier for other countries to make economic contacts, and recently both the United States and Japan have taken extensive advantage of this, as have many Western European powers. Western companies have particularly large sums invested in Southern Africa. In 1965 foreign investment in South Africa alone totalled $4,802 million of which 61 per cent was British, and the next largest share, 11 per cent, American. In addition to these financial involvements, there are political and strategic interests. Along with the rest of the developing world, African states suffer from the conflicts of the major powers, who tend to interpret events everywhere in the context of the cold war. This leads to some absurd misinterpretations. Journalists and politicians describe African affairs simply in terms of a shift to or away from one world power bloc. The West regards with excessive suspicion any departure from traditional capitalism; a communist plot is seen behind every act of nationalization, every programme for social justice.

In the 'Portuguese' territories, the situation is aggravated by Portugal's own position in Europe and in the Western alliances. For Portugal herself is the recipient of massive foreign investment; she is formally a member of EFTA and of NATO.

This whole complex situation is exploited to the full by the

Portuguese government. At a press conference in March 1968 the foreign minister, Alberto Nogueira, made a lengthy statement containing the main points of Portuguese propaganda to the West:

Russia's naval penetration in the Indian Ocean will occupy a great deal of what is abandoned by Britain, and many bases and ports will be denied the West.

We are in Africa because that is our right, our duty and our interest. But we are in Africa because that is also the general interest of the free world.

If the bases and the islands and the ports and airports and the coastlines were not in firm Portuguese hands, one can ask, in whose hands would they be? But in any case those new masters would not offer to the West the guarantees which we, if we want to, will be in a position to offer.

Nogueira has developed this theme extensively in his book, *The Third World*.* In brief the argument runs that independence in colonial territories is followed by chaos, and the threat of communist 'take-over'; that Portugal's African 'provinces' constitute one of the last bastions preserving 'western civilization' in that part of the world, and that it is therefore in the interest of the entire West to help Portugal stay in Africa. This is a straight plea for more Western backing in Portugal's colonial wars. Indeed, this search for support has been the major influence on Portugal's foreign policy from the time of the first outbreak of fighting in Angola in 1961. Since then, foreign investment in the colonies has been deliberately and actively encouraged; bonds have been tightened with the other white régimes in Africa; and the Western allies have been encouraged to extend their military commitments in metropolitan Portugal. As her position in Africa becomes more critical, her statements and appeals have become progressively blunter. There exists a certain doubt, though, about how best to attract foreign support; whether she must inspire confidence in her ability to prevail, or whether she should threaten failure. This must depend to a large extent on how far her various allies accept her predictions of a general disaster following her withdrawal, or on how far they believe that the Portuguese presence serves their own particular interests.

* Johnson Publications, 1968.

It is not surprising that her policy has been most successful with the other minority governments of Southern Africa. Although the Portuguese theory of 'assimilation' differs from the South African doctrine of 'separate development', the practices of the two governments are very similar. Dr Nogueira himself stated, after a visit to South Africa: 'we share and fight for the same principles.' The three main 'white powers' – South Africa, Rhodesia and Portugal – are clearly linked together in a military, political and economic alliance, which may be informal but is rapidly becoming one of the most important elements in the overall situation.

Of these three countries, South Africa is in the strongest position; she is by far the richest country, has the best equipped army and police force, and is at present shielded by the other countries from an independent Africa which might assist her own liberation movements. Portugal and Rhodesia are clearly the potential 'takers' in the alliance. But South Africa has good reason to give. Without the protection of these white buffer states, her own position would be much more difficult to maintain. Her economic interests are also served by maintaining friendly governments in these neighbouring countries.

Mozambique, although not indispensable, is thus important to her. For over fifty years, a large part of her mine labour has been drawn from Mozambique, and her rich gold industry is dependent for its continued profitability on such a source of easily controlled cheap labour. Perry Anderson, in *Portugal et al fin de l'ultracolonialisme*, states the reasons for this:

It is the irrational nature of the gold industry in South Africa which makes this process (contracting of immigrant labour) necessary. The ore on the Rand has such a low gold content and is now only to be found at such depths that under normal conditions its extraction would be a far from economically viable proposition: to get one ton of gold, it is necessary to work about 160,000 tons of ore. Mines where the ore is richer and more accessible have been abandoned in Australia and the United States.

South Africa gains a great deal of her political strength from the fact that she is the world's greatest gold producer. Although her economy would not be overwhelmed by the loss of her gold exports, any threat to her gold industry must be regarded as a serious threat to her delicate political position. Even if she could replace Mozambican labour in the event of its being cut off, she would then become very much more dependent on the remaining sources, and more vulnerable to political changes in the countries of origin.

The economic interests which South Africa now has within Mozambique are also considerable. The most important of these is certainly the Cabora Bassa dam, which will yield high returns on her large capital investment, if the project is ever completed under the present terms.

Her economic interests in Angola are more varied and of longer standing. Also because of her geographical situation, Angola is in a position to affect significantly the question of South West Africa, where extremely important resources are, at the moment, altogether under South African control.

It is hardly surprising, therefore, that in the present situation, South Africa is becoming increasingly involved in the struggles of her neighbours.

The relationship between Mozambique and Rhodesia is much more one of mutual dependence. Since UDI, the existence of a friendly government in Mozambique has been a crucial factor in the ability of the Smith government to evade sanctions. The natural route for Rhodesian trade runs through Mozambique; Beira is the nearest port to Salisbury and Bulawayo; the main river, roads and railways of Rhodesia reach the coast through Mozambique. Mozambique, on her side, profits from all this; 10 per cent of her gross national income is derived from transit services to and from Rhodesia.

Cooperation between the governments of Southern Africa has certainly been increasing since nationalism has become a more immediate threat to the continued dominance of white minorities there. Even before 1964, the Portuguese tended to assume that South Africa would help them in a situation of real danger. In 1964 Wilf Nussy, reporting in the Zambian *Northern News* (24 August 1964) on a visit to Angola, said that he had heard frequently from the Portuguese there the comment, 'Of course, if we have a real war, then the South Africans will come and fight for us.' In the same year, just after the outbreak of the war in Mozambique, Portugal was seeking some diplomatic agreement to substantiate this assumption. The Johannesburg *Star* reported, on 6 October 1964: 'Portugal is ready to sign an agreement with South Africa covering the relations between the two countries, according to reliable sources close to the Portuguese Foreign Minister, Dr Alberto Franco Nogueira.'

In 1965 a commercial agreement between Rhodesia and Portugal was announced, and this was followed by a further series of moves aimed at increasing economic relations between the two countries. In 1965 trade was relatively unimportant; Rhodesia accounted for only 1·9 per cent of Mozambique's imports and 3·1 per cent of her exports. But the following years have seen a concerted effort by both governments to expand it. In 1966 a mission of Portuguese bankers and industrialists visited Rhodesia, and in the same year B. H. Musette, the Rhodesian Minister of Commerce and Industry, made a speech at the Mozambique trade fair calling for 'a major increase in economic relations between Mozambique and Rhodesia'. During the same period a vigorous effort was made to forge stronger political links: in June 1965 Clifford Dupont, the then Rhodesian Defence Minister, visited the Governor-General of Mozambique, Costa Almeida. Two months later Almeida returned the visit and commented: 'In all the events on the official programme for the visit, there was a clear intention to underline the good relations which exist between Mozambique, province of Portugal, and Rhodesia, and on all occasions I received unequivocal proofs of consideration and sympathy.' (*Diário de Moçambique*, 23 August 1965.)

In 1965, representatives of all three countries came together for political discussions, and *Le Monde* reported on 14 September: 'According to information drawn from diplomatic circles in Lisbon, a secret agreement has been signed between Portugal, Southern Rhodesia and South Africa for the defence of white Africa, that is the southern part of the African continent where European domination has survived. ... This agreement allows for the organization of a common defence for Southern Africa against "nationalist and communist subversion".' Links have been tightening since: 1967 saw the final agreement between South Africa and Mozambique on the Cabora Bassa dam; and, on the political front, the South African Defence Minister, Mr Piet Botha, visited Portugal in April for defence talks.

These agreements have already borne some fruit. Rhodesia is certainly gaining help in evading sanctions through her alliance with Mozambique. Mozambique accepts Rhodesian currency and Rhodesian passports, and, according to a report in the *Manchester Guardian* weekly of 12 December 1967, half Rhodesia's oil requirements reach her through Lourenço Marques. It is no secret that there are South African troops and aircraft in Rhodesia, and there is plenty of evidence that in a smaller way Mozambique is receiving military assistance from her. From early on in the war, we have seen and heard of South Africans fighting with the Portuguese, and one guerrilla unit after a battle found a dead soldier with an identification chain on his wrist which showed him to be from South Africa. The Portuguese deserter, Afonso Henriques Sacramento do Rio, stated that he had seen a Southern Rhodesian commander who had come to study anti-guerrilla warfare in the Portuguese army.

There are some pressure groups in South Africa urging closer involvement still in the war in Mozambique. The Durban *Sunday Tribune*, for example, has published a series of features on Mozambique, trying to solicit sympathy for the Portuguese cause and establishing a fund to provide 'comforts' for the Portuguese soldiers, so as to show 'our common aims and purpose to maintain civilization in Southern Africa'. (Aida Parker, 31 December 1967.)

Mr Vorster, South Africa's Prime Minister, made a significant remark in the course of 1967, when questioned on his policy to his northern neighbours:

'We are good friends with both Portugal and Rhodesia. Good friends do not need a pact. Good friends know what their duty is when a neighbour's house is on fire.'

This was made much of in the same *Tribune* article:

Good words, well spoken.

Now let us look at our neighbour Mozambique, a neighbour whose house is certainly on fire in the far north.

Up there in the north 45,000 Portuguese soldiers are fighting, some dying, to hold back the red equipped terrorists seeping in from Tanzania.

The Southern African countries are clearly those most immediately concerned about the outcome of the struggle in the Portuguese territories. Between Portugal and these countries, however, there is, as yet, no official, formal alliance. As a European power on the other hand, Portugal has another set of neighbours, and with these she has an official political and military alliance: NATO. It is to the NATO area that much of Portugal's diplomacy and propaganda is directed.

In theory Portugal's membership of NATO should not affect her African wars, since according to the present terms of the treaty, NATO equipment and finance are for use only within the NATO area, of which the colonies are not a part. In fact Portugal does gain both directly and indirectly from the alliance. First of all, the cost of the Portuguese army in Portugal is covered by NATO, so leaving her free to devote her own military resources to Africa; secondly, her officers are trained by NATO, and there is no ban on such forces going to fight in Africa. Apart from this, in the absence of any efficient check, it is quite possible for her, albeit illegally, to send considerable quantities of NATO weapons, particularly small arms, to Africa; and there is good evidence, provided by the examination of captured weapons, that she does this.

Indirectly, membership of NATO helps Portugal in establishing unilateral links with other member countries, which sell arms to her or help her to manufacture them in Portugal under licence. Since the much publicized Portuguese atrocities in Angola in 1961, these arms agreements have been criticized by liberal opinion in the countries involved, and in some, governments have officially banned the export of arms for use in Africa. In 1961, the British Prime Minister, answering a question in parliament, stated:

In deciding whether to negotiate a sale or to grant a licence for the export of military equipment to Portugal, we have to consider her reasonable military requirements as a NATO ally. But supplies of equipment to Portuguese overseas territories are in a different category, and applications in these cases are for the time being in suspense.

He did not, however, expand on how the British government was to ensure that equipment supplied to Portugal would not be used in Africa.

Similarly, in 1966, the West German Ministry of Defence stated:

The Federal Republic of Germany has sold to Portugal forty surplus planes of the type Fiat G91. The sale took place on the basis of the principle of mutual aid between NATO partners. The delivery is subject to a clause that . . . the planes are to be used exclusively in Portugal for defence purposes within the framework of the NATO pact.

Whatever a British or German government really intends by such statements, it is clear that the Portuguese authorities do not take them in the same spirit as the British or German public is meant to. On the 1966 sale of Fiats, a spokesman for the Portuguese Ministry of Defence commented:

The transaction was agreed within the spirit of NATO. It was agreed that the planes would be used only for defensive purposes within Portuguese territory. Portuguese territory extends to Africa, Angola, Mozambique, Portuguese Guinea.
(*Flying Review International*, April 1966)

NATO itself is somewhat ambivalent on the issue of what precisely constitutes the NATO area. A communiqué from the Ministerial meeting of the NATO Council in December 1957 reported:

We express our interest in the maintenance of peace and conditions of stability and economic and political well-being in the vitally important continent of Africa. We hope that the countries and peoples of that continent who are disposed to do so will cooperate with the free world in efforts to promote these purposes. . . . Historic, economic and other friendly ties between certain European countries and Africa would make such cooperation particularly desirable and effective.

Reading between the lines of this statement, one would scarcely be rash in assuming that some elements in the NATO administration do not examine too closely what Portugal does with the arms she receives.

Even if the NATO powers do not entirely share Nogueira's opinion of the strategic value of Portugal's work in Africa, they certainly seem to be swayed by the strategic value of Portugal herself. France, West Germany and the United States all have bases on Portuguese territory and are expanding military commitment in the area. Two newspaper reports point to a connexion between this and military aid:

France, which sells Portugal the Alouette helicopter used in Africa and is building frigates for her, has been granted a missile tracking station on the Azores. (*The Times*, 24 March 1966)

The retreat from polemics between Americans and Portugal over Africa has contributed to a tacit understanding on quite another matter – keeping American air bases in the Azores . . . the installations and personnel put about $5 million *per annum* into the local Azores economy and since 1957 Portugal has received $300 million in US military aid. . . . The Salazar government will not hesitate to leave NATO and break the link with the US if Portuguese interests in Africa are not upheld. (George Sherman in the *Washington Evening Star*, 20 August 1965)

Apart from her connexion through NATO, Portugal has other close ties with Western Europe. Her 'special relationship' with England goes back as far as the Treaty of Windsor in 1386. She is still reckoned Britain's oldest ally, and traditionally a large portion of her trade has been with Britain. Much of Portugal's existing network of communications was financed by British capital – the Lisbon Electric Tramway Co., with a capital reserve of £7,900,000, is just one example – and a very large part of her industry is partly or wholly British owned. The creation of EFTA and Portugal's admission as a member served to strengthen the existing economic ties with Britain, and in particular have boosted Portuguese exports there; while in 1960 Britain took 13·6 per cent of Portugal's exports, in 1964 she was taking 15·8 per cent.

For Portugal, EFTA's main importance may have been in strengthening this existing link; but it has also served to bring Portugal into closer contact with the other member states. Trade with Sweden has increased significantly, and even more important, a flow of Swedish investment and technical assistance has been facilitated by the EFTA machinery.

The EFTA countries are not, however, the only European powers with important economic interests in Portugal. In recent years West Germany has been a prop of increasing significance. Before the creation of EFTA, West Germany had almost outstripped Britain in the proportion of Portuguese trade she took. In the more modern industries, German capital is at least as important as British; the Grundig factory at Braga and the fibre factory at Oporto indicate the kind of industry that German investors are supporting. Parallel to this recent and rapid expansion of investment, there has been a sharp increase of German military involvement in Portugal, exemplified by the £25 million airforce base at Beja, which is 75 per cent financed by Germany and which is to house German troops and aircraft. The economic assistance itself is in some cases directly related to military aid; one of the more important German factories is an armaments plant at Braço de Prata.

Even where there is no direct link with military needs, the effect of all economic assistance on the war is considerable. Portugal, with one of the lowest economic rates in Europe, a low *per capita* income and a constant shortage of domestic capital, would not have been able to stand the economic strain of the war without the constant injections of foreign capital.

An overtly fascist state, with an outdated administration and an obviously repressive colonial policy, Portugal may at times be an embarrassing ally for the West; but at international gatherings they still treat her as an ally. As such she gains not only material assistance but also diplomatic support. When the question of her colonies has been raised at the United Nations, all the Western Powers, since 1961, have consistently voted with her, against the vast majority of member states. Some of the statements made by Western diplomats specifically point to a link between this political support and the economic commitments already described. In 1967 Mr Garcia for the United States said of the draft resolution being presented to the UN General Assembly:

My delegation . . . has strong reservations regarding the emphasis placed in the draft resolution on factors other than the outmoded

Portuguese policy. In particular the United States is concerned about the stress on the activities of foreign economic and financial interests. It is worth noting that before 1961, the United States had not voted with the other Western allies, but had supported motions condemning Portugal's colonial policy. 1961 was the year when Portugal's new 'open door' policy towards investments in the colonies was beginning to show results.

If the, as yet, relatively modest scale of investment in the Portuguese colonies can affect policy to this extent, it is not surprising that the much larger sums invested in South Africa bias the West even more against movements seeking radical political change in that region of Africa. Since the future of South Africa could be affected by changes in the Portuguese colonies, these important holdings in South Africa bear on Western policy towards Portugal herself.

Western policy on Southern Africa is still marked, however, with ambiguities and divisions. There are politicians who have argued that, in the long run, an attempt to preserve the *status quo* in areas of such extreme racial and social inequality will not benefit the West: on the one hand, it could lead to violence and destruction on such a scale that there would be little left for anyone to salvage; on the other, the ultimate failure of apartheid and fascism backed by the 'democratic' West, would mean a major setback in Western influence throughout the world. There are also individuals and groups who suggest that moral considerations should be given some weight, and who point out that by supporting Portugal and South Africa, the West must forfeit all right to pose as a champion of 'freedom' and 'democracy'. Among these are some church organizations; bodies like the American Committee on Africa; the British and Scandinavian Anti-Apartheid movements; and various liberal and socialist pressure groups. On the other hand, a number of leading politicians have openly and explicitly stated the case for backing the existing régimes. Sir Alec Douglas-Home, former British Prime Minister, visited South Africa early in 1968 and shortly after his return made a speech in which he said:

I made no bones about it that the main purpose of my visit to South Africa was to advance the following thesis and do so in time.

First, that the balance of influence and power in the Middle East, the gateway to Africa, was changing.

Secondly, that the Soviet Union was adopting a new oceanic naval strategy, which would bring her into the West Indian Ocean; and thirdly, that in those circumstances Britain and South Africa had a joint interest in ensuring that the trade routes round Africa were kept open and free. That the Simonstown Agreement was the instrument ready to hand by which to guarantee that security ... (Speech to the South Africa Club dinner, 21 May 1968)

Official government statements, however, are more cautious. Western diplomacy pays lip-service to multi-racialism and democracy, while the governments quietly continue to act against both. Britain reaffirms her alliance with Portugal; she stops selling arms to South Africa, but makes no attempt to reduce other types of trade; she calls for sanctions against Rhodesia, but refuses even to threaten military action and invokes the British interests at stake in South Africa as an excuse; she professes a desire to see majority rule in Rhodesia, but will not even discuss giving assistance to the African organizations who are fighting for exactly this. France steps in to replace Britain as arms supplier to South Africa and sends oil to Rhodesia, while de Gaulle proclaims himself the champion of the Third World. The United States sends arms to Portugal (in 1966 the CIA provided Portugal with seven B26 bombers); West Germany helps her to manufacture her own arms; the United States, France and West Germany all have bases on Portuguese territory; all these countries have large enterprises which are investing vigorously in South Africa, in Portugal, in Mozambique and Angola. Clearly, whatever diplomats may say, the weight of the Western alliance is being thrown behind white dictatorship, against the liberation movements.

Faced with the alliance of the Southern African governments backed by the Western powers, liberation movements must consolidate all forces operating in their favour.

The first and most lasting asset of a liberation movement is the population of the country where it works. The first task is to ensure unity within the movement and among the population. FRELIMO's successes owe a great deal to the fact that there is only one liberation movement in Mozambique, and that within it the people have been able to unite across tribal, religious and other differences. Beyond this, however, unity of action is necessary between all forces fighting the same enemy. In the case of FRELIMO this means, first and foremost, alliance with the liberation movements in the other Portuguese colonies: the MPLA in Angola, and the PAIGC in Guinea Bissau. The concept of such cooperation goes back as far as 1920, when the *Liga Africana* was created in Lisbon among African radical intellectuals of all the territories. By the late fifties, when it was becoming clear that military action would be the only possible road to liberation, a different type of movement was called for, and in 1961 the Conference of Organizations of the Portuguese Colonies (CONCP) was created; FRELIMO joined after its formation in 1962.

The 'Direction Committee' of the CONCP is composed of the supreme leaders of each party, and it meets every six months to arrange the work of the other bodies in the CONCP, the executive secretariat and a number of permanent special commissions. As well as providing a forum for discussion and cooperation, the CONCP carries out work on behalf of the member parties in the fields of research, diplomacy and information. It publishes regular reports on the Portuguese colonies and on the progress of the struggle in each. It coordinates the diplomatic efforts of the parties, enabling the representatives of one to speak for the whole movement at international conferences and within international organizations.

The war is being fought against the existing régime in Portugal, and this régime is in no sense democratic or representative of the ordinary Portuguese people. There is strong underground opposition to the government within Portugal itself, and this provides another field for cooperation; the forces opposing dictatorship in the colonies and the forces opposing dictatorship within Portugal are fighting a common enemy. The Portuguese Liberation Front has an office in Algiers, as does the CONCP, and contact is maintained between them. If a government of a radically different nature were able to replace the dictatorship, it would be possible to gain independence through peaceful negotiation.

Portugal's most immediate allies are South Africa and Rhodesia, and thus the next stage of unity must be unity between the members of CONCP and the forces which are fighting in these countries. The Liberation Committee of the OAU provides a point of contact for all the liberation movements; but as yet there is no closer, overall organizational link, although the interrelation of the nationalist struggles in Southern Africa is being increasingly recognized, and closer cooperation is being achieved between the movements involved. The best example of this is the joint military campaign being undertaken in Rhodesia by the Zimbabwe African Peoples Union (ZAPU) and the African National Congress of South Africa (ANC).

Because of the important part played by the OAU and the independent states which border on the areas of fighting, this question involves the wider one of general African unity. The need for this unity and the factors acting against it raise questions too complex for the scope of this book; but in terms of liberation, there have been some developments worth comment. In recent years the conception of the role to be played in the struggle by independent Africa has changed. During the early years of independence, some of the new African leaders, in particular Kwame Nkrumah, did invaluable work in propagating the ideal of a strong united independent Africa which would pose a formidable threat to remaining minority governments. At that time, however, internal problems and the extent of outside opposition was not fully realized. As the independent states have been getting to grips with the formidable difficulties which face them, a more realistic, if apparently less ambitious, approach has developed. It has been recognized that an all-out offensive against Southern Africa is not the answer. The struggle is one that must be fought from within, making use of guerrilla tactics and based on a pervasive and popular underground movement. The independent states cannot help by direct military intervention but can give much more valuable assistance in the form of material and diplomatic support. The development of political thought in countries such as Tanzania, Guinea, the UAR and Algeria has helped them take a strong lead in this direction. Both the OAU and individual states have also done important work in assisting the achievement of unity within the liberation movements themselves: the refusal to recognize splinter groups, and the efforts made, where more than one major movement already exists, to encourage these to cooperate, have contributed considerably to the struggle. More work needs to be done along these lines, but already there are instances where fragmentation has been prevented by such action. The OAU also helps the liberation movements to get recognition and establish contacts with other parts of Africa. As an organization of governments, the OAU officially excludes liberation movements from its proceedings, but the practice of admitting them as observers has partially overcome this difficulty.

The big powers who have associated themselves with Portugal and South Africa also have interests over the rest of the world, and so all countries which feel themselves to some extent threatened by these interests are natural allies for the liberation movements of Africa. This means primarily the rest of the developing world. FRELIMO and the other members of the CONCP, therefore, have established links with the organizations of the Third World. They all belong to the executive committee of the Afro-Asian Peoples' Solidarity Organization, and the MPLA is also a member of the Secretariat. FRELIMO and other CONCP members are on the secretariat of the Tricontinental Congress and on the executive committee of the World Council of Peace. We have also established relations with many of the countries individually. A particularly fertile exchange of ideas is possible with those countries which, like North Korea, North Vietnam and Cuba, share the problems of the Third World and have also had to fight, or are still fighting, for their national identity as we are doing.

The socialist countries are firm supporters of the liberation movements. FRELIMO has cordial relations with most of them individually, and has received considerable material help.

Although most of the Western governments are not well disposed towards our struggle, many people in the West sympathize with our aims, and we make every effort to establish contact and cooperate with these. In America and Western Europe, organizations concerned with the Third World and church bodies also have helped us with our educational and medical programmes. Even among Western governments there are exceptions: the Scandinavian countries in particular have made considerable contributions to education.

Apart from material aid, diplomatic gains are the most immediate advantages to be gathered from world-wide cooperation. In this field FRELIMO's aims are obviously to isolate Portugal and to win recognition for the liberation movement. Some success can be claimed already, particularly within Africa itself: the African Organization of Telecommunications and the Economic Commission for Africa have decided to exclude Portugal and to admit instead Mozambique, Guinea Bissau and Angola. The OAU has decided that these countries should be represented by their liberation movements, thus giving these further opportunities of working with the rest of Africa on common problems.

The United Nations is obviously an important forum for diplomatic pressure, and 1960 was an extremely important turning point in our relationship with the organization. For in that year the General Assembly decided that the Portuguese 'Overseas Provinces' should be classified as non-self-governing territories.

Portugal had originally been admitted to the UN in 1955, when the General Assembly had accepted her assertion, based on the conversion of her colonies into provinces, that she had no non-self-governing territories. Since its formation, FRELIMO has regularly petitioned before the Committee of Twenty-four on non-self-governing territories, and the committee has submitted motions condemning Portugal, calling for sanctions against her and for support for the work of liberation. These motions have been passed by overwhelming majorities, but the opposition of the West has made it impossible to implement their recommendations. Despite this, the debates have at least helped to disseminate information on the situation and to bring us unilateral aid from a variety of countries. The UN is also another field where the battle for recognition is being fought. In 1966 Mário Andrade, in his capacity as Executive Secretary of the CONCP, put it to the Committee of Twenty-four that Portugal should be regarded not as a nation refusing to implement Resolution 1514 on non-self-governing territories, but as a foreign power trying to prevent, with military force, a people from exercising their right to independence. The acceptance of that proposition would mean that UN sanctions could be ordered against Portugal as an aggressor. In 1967 the Special Committee made a number of recommendations which were designed to enable the bodies of the UN to give assistance to liberation movements where these are engaged in governing and developing a part of their national territory. Associated with this is the effort to prevent Portugal from receiving assistance from international organizations. In particular, the World Bank has been urged not to cooperate with Portugal.

In connexion with this, the question is periodically raised of whether liberation movements should constitute themselves as governments in exile, which might remove some of the mechanical barriers to recognition and membership of international bodies. FRELIMO, however, has opposed this view, on the grounds that it obscures the essential place of liberation movements in world affairs. 'Government in exile' is also a misleading and contradictory title. In the liberated areas of Mozambique, FRELIMO is in fact the government, a government operating within its national territory and not a government in exile. And FRELIMO will not claim to be the government of the whole of Mozambique until all Mozambican nationals can participate in the process of electing that government. The Second Congress showed that we have gone a long way towards fulfilling this condition; but this in itself should give us greater authority in international circles without our having to claim a legally confusing title.

10 The Future

When millet sprouts up in our fields, it is because we had previously prepared the ground and watered the seed with the sweat of our own work. The future is always built on the everyday work of our hands and minds.

1968 New Year message to FRELIMO *militants from the Central Committee*

The disappearance of Dr Salazar as prime minister in Portugal caused a great deal of speculation in the West about the future of Portugal's policy in Africa. Many correspondents suggested that the change might open the way to some kind of peaceful solution. We never shared this optimism. For, although it had all the appearances of a personal dictatorship, the Salazar régime was really an oligarchy. The personality of the dictator moulded the external appearance of the government; but the power behind was that of a small group of big landowners, industrialists and military leaders. Caetano's authority as Salazar's successor rests on this same base, and therefore even if he wished to, he would find it virtually impossible to make major changes in a direction which would jeopardize the interests of this powerful minority. In fact there was little in Caetano's political record to suggest that he would wish to change the existing structure in any of its essentials. He himself had taken an important part in the building of the Salazar state; he had been the theoretician, the legal mind behind it, and one of the most inventive apologists for Portuguese colonial policy. Our judgement was confirmed within the next few months by the announcement that yet more troops were to be sent to Guinea, followed shortly by a clear statement from Caetano that policy in Africa would remain unchanged.

Some journalists have also suggested that, even though the

succession of Caetano may not bring about a change of policy by the existing government, it may precipitate violent upheavals in Portugal itself which would affect the situation in Africa. Even under Salazar, the Portuguese state was not as monolithic as it appeared. There were factions within the government; Moreira's movement in the early sixties was just one instance that was not entirely hidden from public view. There has always been, too, a more radical opposition by illegal antifascist parties, operating in exile and underground in Portugal. If the present machinery of oppression were seriously weakened, these would certainly try to take advantage of the situation, and if they could succeed in gaining power, we are convinced that they would discuss the question of independence with us. Unfortunately such an outcome seems to us, at the moment, highly improbable, because of the immense strength of the army and the police: if major divisions did develop within the ruling group they would be more likely to result in a new army coup and in the establishment of an emergency military dictatorship.

We can, therefore, see no alternative in the near future to continuing with the war. The question is, for how long? Portugal is one of the poorest countries in Europe, and she has a population of only 9 million. Already she has 150,000 troops overseas and spends nearly half her revenue on the war. Both the number of troops being sent abroad and the defence budget have been increasing rapidly in the last few years. The effects of the war are being felt more than ever inside Portugal. Apart from the extension of national service and the increase in taxation, which hit most heavily the poorest and least powerful section of the population, there has been a general economic set-back which is causing concern among top Lisbon businessmen and industrialists. Up to about 1966, the war had had the effect of apparently stimulating the economy, but by 1967 the real position was beginning to show. The increase in national income, noticeable in the early sixties, was due partly to the government's intensive drive for foreign investment and partly to the normal impact of a war in creating a sudden increase of demand. In a country as underdeveloped as Portugal, however, much of this demand can only be met by foreign goods, and the increasing pressure on home production exercised by the unproductive requirements of war, is beginning to tell.

Added to the economic strain of the war, is the fact that, despite the enormous effort she is making, Portugal is slowly losing. Most of Guinea is now controlled by the PAIGC, and fighting is slowly spreading in Angola and Mozambique.

These factors have created doubts at the highest level. Salazar himself admitted, about six months before his stroke (11 January 1968): 'If the troubles there (in the African Provinces) continue very much longer, they will diminish our ability to carry on.' Yet the determination to carry on is unchanged. The Foreign Minister, Nogueira, stated unequivocally in *The Third World*: 'In the entire world, even among our adversaries and critics, no one expects us to alter our policy, no one believes that we shall alter it, and our position is considered to be firm and final.' The divisions within the government are not based on whether to continue the war, but on how to continue it, and this boils down to the problem of aid. Without the economic and military support which Portugal receives from the West and in particular from South Africa, Portugal's war effort would probably have collapsed already. Of her various allies, South Africa is the most promising, since the future of Mozambique might well affect the future of South Africa's own apartheid policy. Yet the more that Portugal relies on South Africa, the more influence South Africa gains over her and her African territories. Although both are police states, the two countries have little in common beyond this and their shared desire to continue their domination over the black African. Both in Portugal and in South Africa there is no consensus about the extent and nature of the association between the two countries.

Lisbon also has to face a certain pressure from the whites in the colonies, a pressure now related to the issue of South African intervention.

Even among the whites in the colonies there are factions. For a long time there has been a body of opinion which resented the tight control exercised by the Metrópole over its 'overseas citizens' and above all the high taxes which have to be paid to the Central Government. Now that they need the Portuguese army to ensure the continuation of their privileges, such dissidents have kept fairly quiet recently; but if the Portuguese army should prove inadequate to the task, they might press for some alternative solution, like a close association with South Africa. Then there are those who have been advocating a neo-colonial solution, independence under a puppet African leader who would leave privileges and economic interests untouched. The politician Cunha Leal, a member of the 'legal opposition' in Lisbon, has been pressing this point of view. There is little prospect, though, that a solution will come out of any such groups alone.

Certainly, there was logic in Salazar's stand against the 'legal opposition'. For with her weak economy, Portugal would be unable to maintain her interests in a neo-colonial situation; the past pattern of colonial government has not created a strong African privileged middle class who could securely take over; the loss of the African territories would undermine the political and economic basis of the present state. Puppet African leaders have already been used to try to undermine the authority of FRELIMO in certain districts, and we can expect to see this technique applied more widely yet; but it is very unlikely that Lisbon would go as far as to grant nominal independence to the whole country.

On the other hand, the links with South Africa will almost certainly grow stronger, and the real extent of them will depend more on South Africa's view of the situation than on Portugal's. Increasing military aid from South Africa cannot but make a difference to the progress of the war, but we do not believe that it will alter the ultimate course. South Africa's army is well trained and well equipped; but it is considerably smaller than Portugal's African army, and a large part of it is permanently tied down in South Africa and South West Africa, while at present a part of it is busy helping the Rhodesian army. Our guerrillas are now sufficiently well organized to meet the threat of limited South African participation in the war, and South Africa is not in a position to concentrate her full armed strength in Mozambique, even if she wished to do so.

Although we are gradually winning the war and have every reason to believe that we will go on winning, we are well aware that final victory is a long way off. For Portugal does have a number of advantages. She has a huge army equipped with modern weapons; in Mozambique there are at least 60,000 fully armed Portuguese soldiers, as against our present army of about 8,000 guerrillas, many of whom are provided with only the bare minimum of equipment and with inadequate weapons. Portugal enjoys the full support of South Africa, the richest country on the continent, and gets useful aid and support from all the rich countries of the West.

Certain geographical and social factors also count in her favour. Mozambique is a huge country, and as we liberate more areas and extend the fighting regions, communication becomes increasingly difficult. This is one reason why we can press on only slowly. For as the frontier of action is pushed forwards, supply lines must be properly organized behind it. In this and every other sphere, the lack of educated personnel hits us. Inefficiency is one of our biggest problems and arises both because people have not had organizational training and because they have not had the political education to understand why certain things have to be done. Thus, before we can operate with a minimum of efficiency in a new region, a major educational drive has to take place.

Paradoxically, the fact that the war will be drawn out in this way may in the long run be an advantage to our ultimate development. For war is an extreme of political action, which tends to bring about social change more rapidly than any other instrument; and in a country as backward as Mozambique, rapid social change will be essential after independence.

Yet for the present, the war is an agony; it makes people homeless, causes famines, diverts energy and talent away from development projects; because of it, people die and are injured. We do not choose war as our path to national independence. War was forced on us. But since at the present moment we have no choice, it is worth recognizing and trying to exploit the constructive aspects of armed struggle.

Liberation is to us not simply a matter of expelling the Portuguese: it means reorganizing the life of the country and setting it on the road to sound national development. Taking political power out of the hands of the Portuguese is a necessary condition for this, since the Portuguese have consistently opposed social progress and have encouraged only those economic developments which could benefit a small, almost entirely foreign élite. But the liberation movement will not be able to claim success until, through it, the people achieve what the Portuguese denied them: a tolerable standard of living; education; the conditions for economic and cultural development; the opportunity to participate in their own government. Thus the question 'How long will the armed struggle last?' is not as important as it seems to be. Whatever happens, whether we have to go on for ten or twenty years, fighting our way inch by inch down to Lourenço Marques, or whether the Portuguese give up and move out within the next few years, our problems will not end with independence. If the war has been long, however, these may be less acute. For the achievement of independence in itself does not change overnight the attitudes of the people, and colonial rule essentially discourages all the qualities which make for successful democracy. Among the uneducated, authoritarian rule discourages initiative, a sense of personal responsibility, and breeds instead an attitude of non-cooperation with government; among the educated few, it encourages an élitism imitated from the elaborate hierarchy of colonial government. In the liberated areas, these are the sort of influences we have had to combat at the same time as campaigning against traditional problems such as tribalism, superstition and the general low level of political and economic understanding. The urgency produced by war conditions has forced us to recognize these problems very early and shown us the enormous importance of political education. As a result, attitudes are beginning to change in the liberated areas. There are still local divisions, misunderstandings, some corruption, and a great deal of sheer inefficiency; but these are decreasing. People are beginning to realize that their future is now in their own hands. This is why we can view the long war ahead of us with reasonable calm. If the Portuguese government were to hand over Mozambique tomorrow, this work would still have to be begun in all the rest of the country; if they hang on for another five years, another ten, or more, it will have gone much further.

Since the point of the war is to build a new Mozambique, not just to destroy the colonial régime, we must all have ideas about how the future nation should be organized; but the issue is too far in the future for us to be able to discuss it formally at this stage. Our policy on immediate questions can give some sort of indication for the future. The structure of FRELIMO can also be regarded as the precursor of a national political body. It is the essence of this structure, however, that ideas should come from the people; that the personnel of the executive and Central Committee are freely elected and may therefore change. The electorate is growing all the time as new areas are liberated and new leaders are emerging at all levels. In ten years' time, the whole executive body may have changed. Thus, in discussing the future any further, I can only voice my own private convictions; I cannot predict what will be decided by a Central Committee which does not yet exist.

The government of any developing country has as its official aim the achievement of broadly based economic and social progress. I believe that one of the necessary conditions for this is to eliminate social and economic forces which favour minorities. By this I mean not just racial minorities: these will automatically lose their special privileges with the establishment of an African State. In many respects, a greater danger lies in the formation of new African privileged groups; the educated as opposed to the uneducated, factory workers as opposed to peasants. Paradoxically, to prevent concentration of wealth and services in small areas of the country and in the hands of a few, strong central planning is needed. This would make it possible to distribute teachers and doctors throughout the country simply by not allowing too many job opportunities in any one area. Similarly, industrial planners could be forced to take into account the labour force, not just the convenience of material transport; new industries would be spread over the country where there are people to work in them, rather than sited in existing towns which are already years in advance of the rural areas. Prices and wages could be regulated over the country as a whole. These measures in themselves would help to even out the distribution of income. But, in addition, it would be necessary to keep a low ceiling on salaries. This is particularly important in the case of government personnel. For, once the people with power in a country enjoy a privileged economic position, they cease to share the problems that they are responsible for solving.

Rapid economic development will be necessary in order to realize any of the social plans. Agriculture will have to be improved, and numerous small processing industries started, so that we can satisfy our own essential needs and reduce imports. However, I do not think that this has to take precedence over plans for mineral extraction and the establishment of heavy industry. These may be slowed to begin with by the necessity to plan so that the benefits will be properly distributed, and they will almost certainly be hampered by our lack of trained personnel; but they will not be neglected because of any theory about the primacy of agricultural development.

In education, also, two parallel programmes, I believe, will be needed. On the one hand, there should be a massive campaign directed at adults as well as children to give the whole population a minimum standard of education. Public hygiene, basic politics, economics and literacy would form the main content of this programme. On the other hand, it will be essential to provide specialized technical courses for a few people, in order to train the personnel needed for running the various development projects. The important thing here is, first of all, that the courses should be closely related to the needs of Mozambique; and, secondly, that the few selected to study to this level should not be permitted other special privileges over and above the clear privilege of higher education.

It will not be easy to realize the type of progress described, and I have set down these ideas only as a rough guide of how I myself see our struggle continuing after we have won the war.

Now, in the present, most of our energies have to be directed towards winning this war. One thing only is certain: that the clock cannot be turned back now. The changes that have taken place in the north cannot be reversed; and, even in the south, where we are not yet physically fighting, the myth of Portuguese strength has been destroyed. The very fact that in over a fifth of the country the colonial state has been eliminated, has already radically changed prospects for the whole of Mozambique and perhaps even in the long run for the whole of Southern Africa.